Skirts

DRESSMAKING **3**

Maureen Goldsworthy

Mills & Boon Ltd
London   Sydney   Toronto

I am most grateful to Rosamund Keer and my daughter Alice Helps, who modelled the skirts. I should also like to thank Robert Saunders of Wright Photography for the photographs, taken at Warwick Castle by kind permission of Warwick Castle Ltd.

For K.R.G.

First published 1980

© Maureen Goldsworthy 1980

ISBN 0 263 06427 1

Designed by Richard Brown Associates

Printed in Great Britain by
Fletcher & Son Ltd, Norwich

and bound by
Richard Clay (The Chaucer Press) Ltd,
Bungay, Suffolk

for the publishers Mills & Boon Ltd,
15–16 Brooks Mews,
London W1Y 1LF

CONTENTS

INTRODUCTION   4

MATERIALS NEEDED FOR PATTERN DRAFTING   5

PERSONAL MEASUREMENT CHART   6

DRAFTING THE BLOCKS   7
Drawing curves   Folding in darts   Drafting the back
block   Drafting the front block   Transferring the
blocks to card

DESIGNING THE PATTERN   12
The draft pattern   The length   The seams   Flared
skirts   Skirts with godets   Pleated skirts   Gathered
skirts   Draped skirts   Wrapover skirts   Pockets
The opening and waist finish   The lining   Seam and
hem allowances   Fabric requirements

MAKING UP THE SKIRT   50
Cutting out   Marking   Before fitting   Fitting
After fitting   Finishing the skirt

INTRODUCTION

Of all garments, skirts may well be the most exciting to design, giving plenty of scope and space for developing the style you choose. They are also the easiest to make, with none of the usual dressmaking headaches over collar or sleeves.

A skirt designed to your own measurements will fit you perfectly because the pattern will be right. The stock sizes of ready-made skirts allow your hips to be 26 cm larger than your waist; unless your measurements obligingly correspond, even an expensive skirt will hang badly. The cost of buying provides an extra incentive to make your own. So if you have had no time for dressmaking since leaving school, a skirt would be the ideal starting-point.

The first section of this book gives instructions for drafting the basic block patterns from your own measurements. All your future skirt patterns, of whatever style, are derived from the permanent record of the blocks. The next part shows how to translate the blocks into a detailed working pattern for the design you have chosen – whether it be pencil-slim or circular, fully-pleated, gathered or draped. Lastly, there are instructions for making up the skirt you have designed.

None of this is difficult, though to begin with it does take a little time. You will probably need an hour to draft the blocks, then another couple of hours to make the final pattern with all the styling details. But if you can follow an ordinary dressmaking pattern, you should have no difficulty with these instructions.

Paper
Squared dressmaker's paper may be difficult to find and is expensive. The plain variety comes in sheets that are too wide for easy handling. It is much better to use a roll of ceiling lining paper. This is strong, easily obtainable and quite wide enough. Besides, you will need plenty of it and it is cheap.

Thin card
Obtainable from art stationers. Two large sheets will be needed for the final pattern blocks.

Set square
This is handy but not essential. Without one, lines at exact right angles to the edge of the paper can be made by creasing. When you fold across the width of the paper, keep the side edges exactly level with each other; the creases will then be at right angles to the side edges (*Figure 1*). Any tendency for the paper to curl up can be cured by pressing with a cool iron.

Tracing wheel
A wheel with sharp metal points, used to transfer pattern outlines from an upper to a lower sheet of paper. Obtainable in haberdashery (US notions) departments (*Figure 2*). A plastic wheel will not do.

Carbon paper
This is for transferring double-thickness markings.

Pencils
Hard pencils (H or 2H). Coloured fibre-tip pens are also useful.

Long ruler or straight edge

Tape measure
This should be marked in centimetres. If you have not yet tried working in centimetres, now is the time to do so. The metric system is actually much easier to use than the imperial system, and you should not attempt to convert one to the other; this is why alternative inch measurements are not given. Just take the centimetres as they come – one soon gets over the shock of one's hip measurement hovering around the hundred mark.

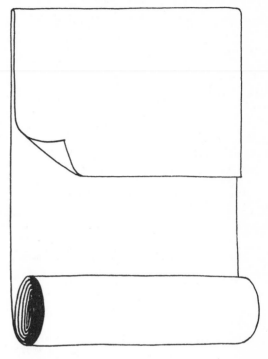

Figure 1

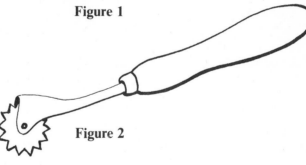

Figure 2

PERSONAL MEASUREMENT CHART

Five body measurements are needed for constructing the skirt pattern blocks; you may as well take the sixth now, and record it for future reference. You must have the help of a friend to measure you – it is impossible to do this accurately for yourself.

Measurements should be taken closely but not tightly. The extra ease needed for movement in the skirt should not be allowed for as it is built into the block patterns (*Figure 3*).

1 Waist, taken firmly at the natural waistline_____cm
Quarter waist measurement_____cm

2 High hip, taken 10 cm below the natural waistline_____cm
Quarter high hip measurement_____cm

3 Hip, taken over the widest part of the hip, usually 20–22 cm below the waist_____cm
Quarter hip measurement_____cm

4 Hip depth The measurement from the waist down to the widest part of the hip, taken down the side seam_____cm

5 Waist to knee length, taken down the side seam_____cm

6 Waist to floor length, taken down the side seam_____cm

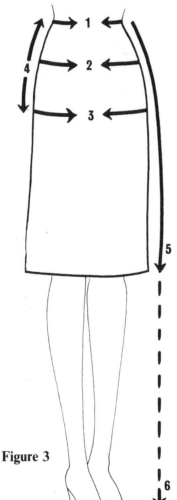

Figure 3

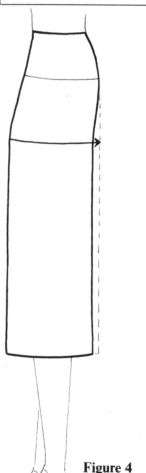

Figure 4

Block patterns are not fashion shapes, and contain no styling. Nor do they include seam and hem allowances: so they cannot be used directly as dressmaking patterns. They are simply the essential record of your bone structure, from which the final pattern is built. Even changes in your weight will not substantially affect the fit. A couple of centimetres more, or less, on hip or waist just means that you need to add or subtract a quarter of that amount on the side seams of the final pattern – which you can do without cutting a new block.

There are two exceptions to this. In larger sizes, the level for the hip measurement may come rather low if the greater width is round the seat, below rather than across the abdomen. In this case the measurement, if taken closely, may pull in the finished skirt when seen from the side – an ugly line and a common fault in jersey skirts (*Figure 4*). To avoid this, have the hip measurement taken loosely enough at the front to allow the skirt you are wearing, while being measured, to hang straight. The extra girth needed may be 2–4 cm. The same applies where a prominent abdomen gives a larger than usual measurement at high hip level; the remedy is the same.

DRAWING CURVES

Pattern drafting consists mainly of measuring and ruling straight lines, but sometimes you will need to draw a curve to connect three or more points. Here is the simplest way to draw a smooth curve.

Always draw from the inside of the curve, so that the movement of your hand goes naturally with the line rather than against it. If you draw as shown in *Figure 5*, you will have less control over your pencil and the line may wobble. But turn the paper round, draw as shown in *Figure 6*, and the movement of your hand will then assist the curve.

For a full curve, rest the heel of your hand on the paper and use it as a pivot. For a very shallow curve, use your elbow as a pivot. Draw quickly; the curve will be smoother than if you tense your fingers and go slowly.

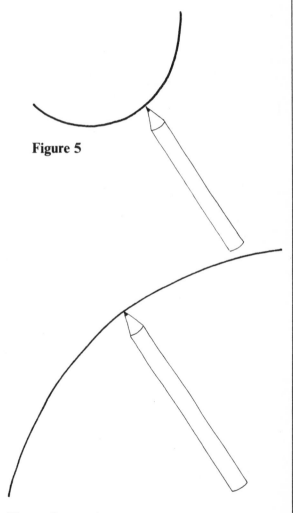

Figure 5

Figure 6

FOLDING IN DARTS

It is easy to draw in the two sides of a dart; less easy to shape the seamline from which the dart springs. The following method is foolproof and should be used for darts in any part of the skirt.

1 Draw in the provisional seamline, usually the waistline, as a straight line A–B shown in *Figure 7*. Mark in the two sides of the dart, C–D and E–D.

2 Lay the paper across the corner of a table, with the lower part of the pattern hanging over the edge. With the point of the dart, D, on the corner of the table, crease the pattern from C to D and bring the crease over to the line E–D, matching the sides of the dart accurately (*Figure 8*).

3 This folding will bend the seamline; so, still with the dart folded, rule a new straight line or draw a shallow curve between A and B. Cut along this line and unfold the dart. *Figure 9* shows the shape of the final seamline.

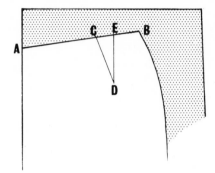

Figure 7

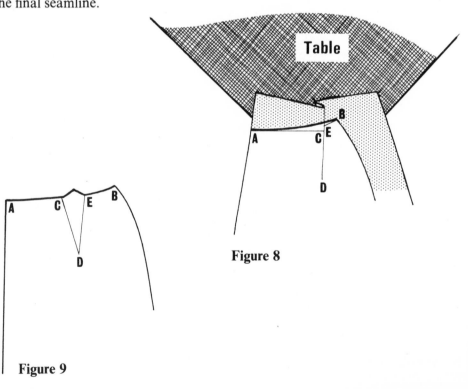

Figure 8

Figure 9

DRAFTING THE BACK BLOCK

Cut two rectangles of paper, one for the back and the other for the front block. Mark the back block as shown in *Figure 10*.

Length: waist to knee length, plus 1 cm.
Width: quarter hip measurement, plus 3 cm.
For the back block:

Mark A, 1 cm below the top left-hand corner.

Measuring down the left-hand edge:

A–B is 10 cm;
A–C is hip depth.

Crease right across the paper from B and C. Mark D at the bottom left-hand corner, E at the bottom right-hand corner and F at the top right-hand corner.

For the waistline and darts

Join A–F.

Measuring along A–F:

A–G is quarter waist plus 4·5 cm (provisional waistline);
A–H is one third of A–G;
H–J is one third of A–G.

Measuring along the line from C:

C–K is quarter hip plus 1 cm;
C–L is one third of C–K;
L–M is one third of C–K.

Join H–L and J–M. Down these lines:

N is 14 cm below H;
P is 12 cm below J.

Mark Q and R, 1 cm to each side of H; join Q–N–R for one dart.

Mark S and T, 1 cm to each side of J; join S–P–T for the other dart.

Fold in the darts as shown in *Figure 8* and draw a shallow curve for the final waistline, across the folds. Cut along this line, and unfold.

For the side seam

Along the line from B, measure:

quarter high hip measurement, plus 1 cm, plus

the width taken out by the darts at this level. This total gives the length of the line B–U.

Join G–U–K–E for the side seam; G–U–K may be slightly curved, but K–E is a straight line. The whole line should be smoothly shaped.

Cut out, discarding the shaded areas shown on the diagram.

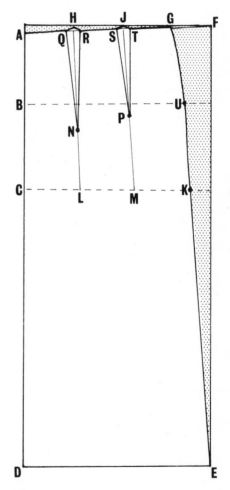

Figure 10

DRAFTING THE FRONT BLOCK

Take the other rectangle of paper.

Lay the back block over it, matching the left and lower edges.

Trace the line E–K and mark in the points A, B, C, F and M as shown in *Figure 11*. Remove the back block.

Join A–F.

Crease across the paper from B.

For the waistline and dart
Measuring along A–F:

A–G is quarter waist plus 2·5 cm;
A–H is two-thirds of A–G.

Join H–M.

Mark J where H–M crosses the line from B.

Mark L and N, 1 cm to each side of H.

Join L–J–N for the dart.

Fold in the dart as before and draw a shallow curve for the final waistline, across the fold.

For the side seam
Along the line from B, measure quarter high hip measurement plus 1 cm and mark P.

To complete the side seam, join G–P–K for the hip curve.

Cut out, discarding the shaded areas. Mark a fold arrow down the left-hand edge.

TRANSFERRING THE BLOCKS TO CARD

Now that the block patterns have been drafted, you should transfer their outlines on to sheets of thin card.

Place the draft of the back block over a sheet of card and run the tracing wheel accurately round its outline. This will prick a line of perforations through the card. Mark in the dart lines and hip level C–K.

Cut out the block.

Cut notches at C and K, to act as balance marks on the final pattern.

Mark in a straight-grain arrow parallel to the left (centre-back) edge.

Repeat this for the front block. Mark heavily so that the perforations will show on the reverse of the card. Now turn the card over and mark the lines on the reverse, so that the two blocks will both relate to the right-hand side of the body.

Cut out the front block. Cut a notch at K. Mark a fold arrow down the right (centre-front) edge.

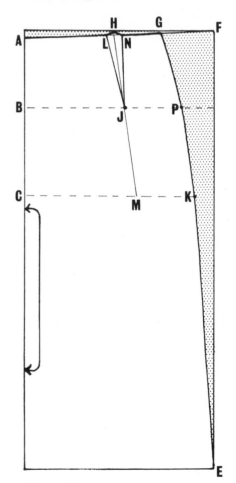

Figure 11

DRAFTING THE BLOCKS

The blocks are now ready to be used for developing whatever style of skirt you may want (*Figure 12*). They themselves are not working patterns, but templets; they are never cut or altered in any way. The final pattern, with all the design details as well as the seam and hem allowances, will be traced from them.

The blocks should last indefinitely. Drafting them is a once-for-all operation. To store them, punch a hole near the top of each block, thread a piece of tape through the holes and hang them from a coathanger. As your collection of block patterns for different types of garment grows, the hangers can be hung flat at the back of a wardrobe where they will take up no space.

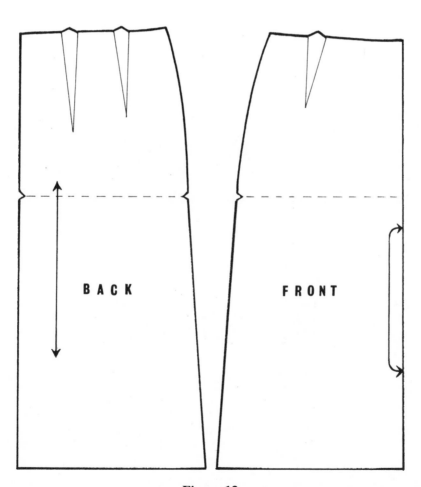

Figure 12

DESIGNING THE PATTERN

With the blocks safely drafted, you are now ready to develop the design for a skirt in whatever style you wish, from mini to floor length.

This section gives instructions for cutting a wide variety of styles. Rather than read the whole section, it is suggested that you just browse through the diagrams for ideas. *Figure 13* shows a group of body outlines; on thin paper placed over these, you could trace and sketch out the effect of various pleating arrangements, different styles of draping, or altered positions for seams – until you have evolved a complete design. Then, simply pick out the instructions for the particular details you need, and disregard the rest.

Take plenty of time deciding; it is quite easy at this stage to work out a pattern for any design – much more difficult, and possibly wasteful in material, to change your ideas later on.

THE DRAFT PATTERN
You do not use the blocks directly as patterns. You draw round their outlines on fresh paper and on those add any styling you want. This often means cutting the draft pattern (not the block) into pieces, to add a yoke seam or to introduce fullness into any part of the skirt; if so, the final outline is drawn round the cut pieces on yet another sheet of paper. Lastly, seam and hem allowances are added and the final pattern cut out. An example of the whole process is given below, and shows the development of the pattern for the simple, knife-pleated skirt on page 19.

THE LENGTH
The blocks are drafted to knee length. There is no change of line below the knee, so no point in making them longer. But you are unlikely to want a skirt cut exactly to the knee, so you should first decide the finished length of the skirt and extend the side and centre lines accordingly. This is partly in order to begin working out the pattern on a long enough piece of paper. Much more important, the length of the skirt will be the main influence on the design; you cannot safely mark in pleats, or the fullness given by drapery or gathers, until you can visualize the length to which they will fall.

The development of a pleated skirt pattern from the basic blocks

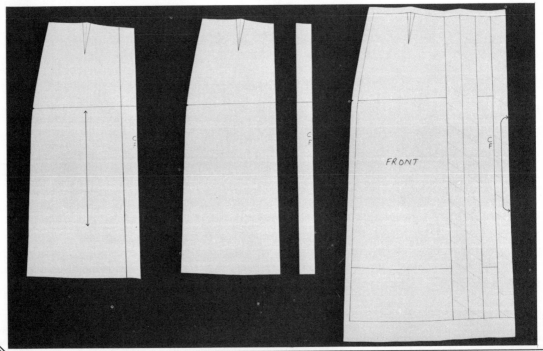

DESIGNING THE PATTERN

At this stage a great aid to designing would be a long, plainly-cut skirt in a dark colour, on which you could chalk a length and try it on to see the effect. If you have such a skirt, it will also be very useful for planning the positions of vertical seams, or the depth and shape of a yoke or pockets. Seen on the body, these tend to look quite different from their drawn lines on paper.

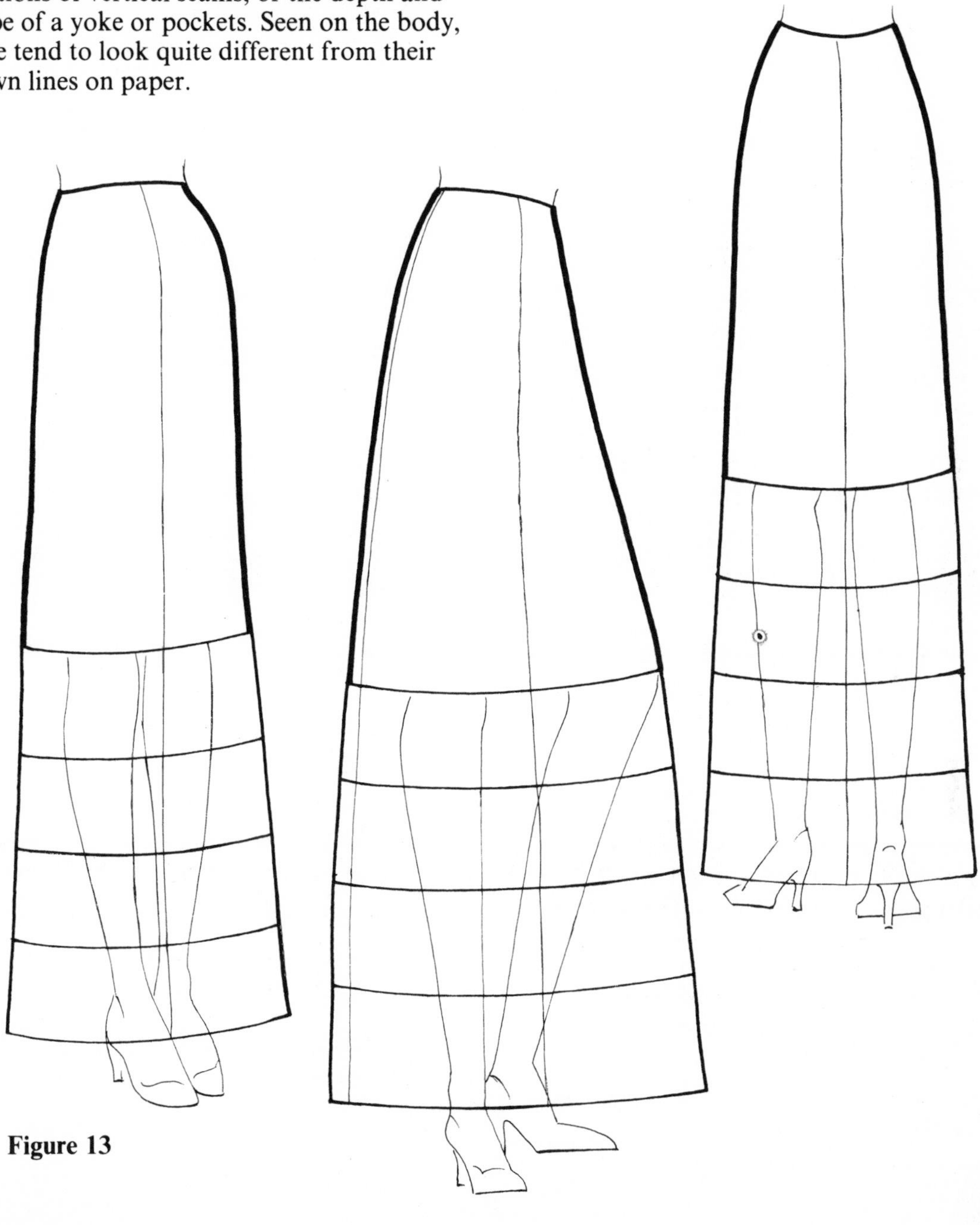

Figure 13

DESIGNING THE PATTERN

THE SEAMS

Whatever type of fullness you intend to have, first plan the seamlines. This is particularly vital if you will be introducing any draping, because that must spring from a seam. Pleats may be more easily managed if they come between seams.

The blocks give a centre-back seam (as the simplest position for a zipped opening) and side seams. But you can equally well cut a one-piece back and place the zip at the side. Or, if you want a front zip, you could add a centre-front seam.

Straight skirt

Without alteration, the blocks can be used for a straight, fitted skirt. The very slight flare from the hipline will make the skirt appear to hang straight; one that was actually cut the same width at hip and hem would seem to taper in. There will be enough striding room for comfort unless cut very long, in which case it will need a slit or kick-pleat.

So for an absolutely plain, straight skirt, trace round the back and front blocks on fresh paper, adding whatever length you want by extending the lines of centre and side seams (*Figure 14*). Do not cut out yet, as at a later stage you will be adding seam and hem allowances.

Panelled skirt

By dividing the front and back each into three panels, you can obtain the very useful six-piece skirt pattern (*Figure 15*). This is one of the best shapes for introducing flare, or inverted pleats. The distance apart of the side-front seams has to be nicely judged; they look better if they are set just forward from the waistline dart position. In this case, the darts would be moved over and redrawn into the top of the seam.

1 On fresh paper, trace round the front block, omitting the dart shaping.

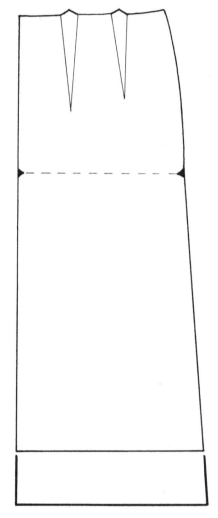

Figure 14

DESIGNING THE PATTERN

2 Draw in the line of the new seam.

3 Draw in the dart, 10 cm long and 2 cm wide, on the seamline. Mark notches as in *Figure 16*.

4 Cut out the draft pattern and cut down the new seamline, trimming off the sides of the dart.

5 Mark a straight-grain arrow on the side-front, parallel to the side-front seam. (If you wish to add any fullness to the pattern, leave out the arrow for the moment; the placing of the fullness may affect its line.) Mark a fold arrow down the centre-front.

6 Repeat for the back pattern, moving the width of both darts into the new side-back seam (*Figure 17*).

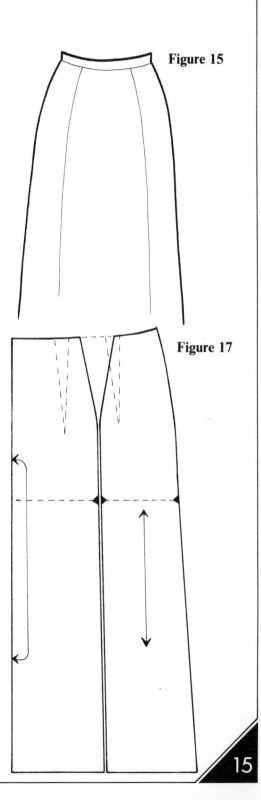

Figure 15

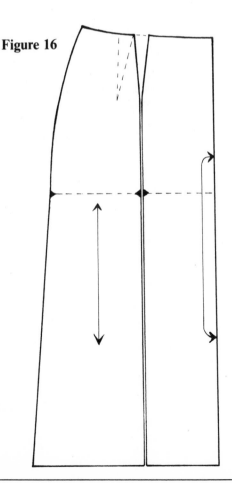

Figure 16

Figure 17

15

DESIGNING THE PATTERN

Skirts can be in as many panels as you wish –
ten or twelve-gored skirts are usually cut to
include a wide flare. But panels need not
necessarily be vertical; the seams can run
diagonally across a skirt and may form the
line from which gathering or a flare or pleats
can spring (*Figure 18*).

Yokes

Yokes are just seams across the skirt at or
above the hipline. Along their lower edge,
they may be cut to any shape, and they can
form a setting for gathers (as in the
photograph on page 37), for pleats or for a
flare (*Figure 19* and the skirt shown on this
page).

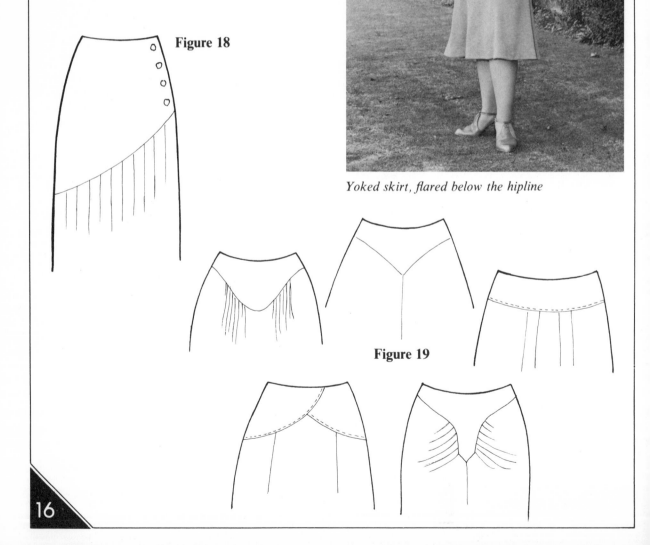

Yoked skirt, flared below the hipline

Figure 18

Figure 19

DESIGNING THE PATTERN

The most pleasing depth for a yoke is difficult to judge on paper – chalk the proposed line on an existing skirt, to help you to decide.

1 Trace round the block and mark the yoke seam (*Figure 20*).

2 Cut off the yoke (*Figure 21*).

3 Close the dart. On fresh paper, draw round the altered yoke outline. Mark a fold arrow at the centre (*Figure 22*).

FLARED SKIRTS

So far, we have been looking only at the line of a seam as it will hang on the figure, without considering any fullness in the skirt.

A flare can be introduced by cutting the draft pattern into a number of panels, and flaring each panel out from the hipline or from lower down the skirt, along each seamline (*Figure 23*). Or the back and front can be cut as single pieces shaped to include the flare. The extreme case is a skirt cut fully circular from the waist.

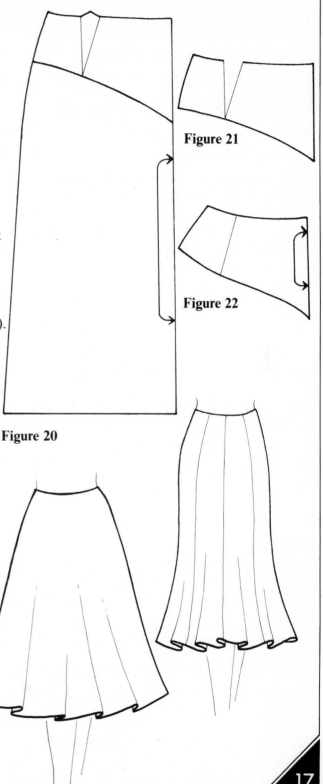

Figure 21

Figure 22

Figure 20

Figure 23

DESIGNING THE PATTERN

Plain flare from the waist

First decide the finished hem width you want, and divide this measurement by four.

1 Draw round the front block, to make the draft pattern.

2 Cut out, then cut into four equal sections (*Figure 24*).

3 Cut out the dart shaping.

4 Over fresh paper, place the waist ends of the sections touching, with the sides of the dart together. You may need to use two widths of drafting paper, sellotaped (US scotch-tape) together.

5 Spread apart the hem ends, leaving equal spaces between them. Redraw a new side seam, half a space out from the old one, as shown in *Figure 25*. The new hem measurement of the pattern should be a quarter of the total hem width. The example shown here will make a very full skirt, about a semicircle.

6 Draw round the new outline. Mark a fold arrow.

7 Repeat for the back block.

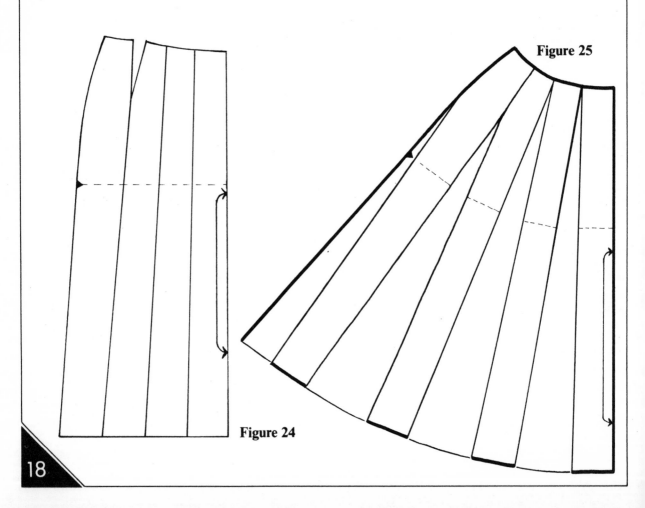

Figure 24

Figure 25

DESIGNING THE PATTERN

Flare from one point at the waistline

Instead of being spread equally all round the skirt, the whole flare can be concentrated at one point, such as at the centre-front. This is especially effective in soft, thin fabrics such as silky jerseys.

Do not cut the pattern into sections; just add the extra hemline width to the centre-front, making the new centre-front line the same length as the old. The dart is not affected (*Figure 26*).

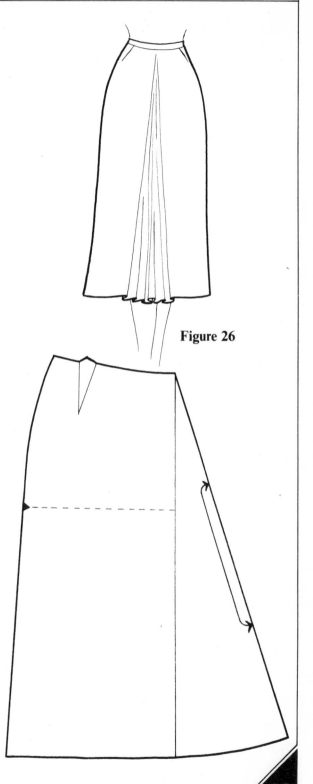

Figure 26

'Beginner's' skirt with unpressed pleats, made from the pattern on page 12

Four-gore skirt

A slightly flared skirt will hang better if made in four gores, with a centre-front seam.

1 Trace round the front block. Rule a line down from the point of the dart, parallel to the centre-front. Cut down this line and cut out the dart shaping.

2 Match the two sections along the sides of the dart. This will add fullness at the hemline (*Figure 27*).

3 Draw the new outline, adding 5 cm at the side seam.

4 Repeat for the back, cutting down from both darts and adding the same width at the hemline as you added to the front (*Figure 28*). (Because of the extra flare at the hip, it does not matter if the points of the darts overlap slightly.)

5 Mark straight-grain arrows down the *centre* of each pattern. The centre-front and centre-back seams will now be on the bias, and this lets the skirt hang more softly.

6 Mark notches on the seamlines at hip level.

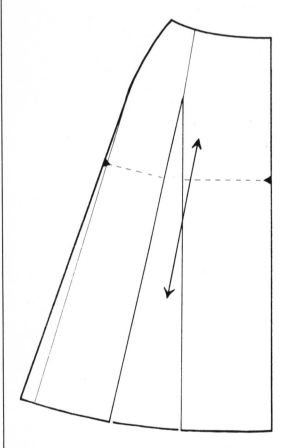

Figure 27

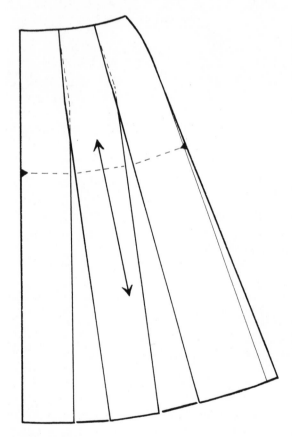

Figure 28

Circular skirt

This is not developed from the block, but based only on your waist measurement.

1 Sellotape two lengths of paper together, to get enough width for drafting the pattern.

2 Mark A at the top left-hand corner (*Figure 29*).

3 Measuring down the left-hand edge: A–B is one-sixth waist measurement; B–C is finished skirt length.

4 Put a pin through your tape measure at the length of A–B. Pin through to A on the pattern. Swing the end of the tape measure round in an arc, marking the waistline curve as you go (*Figure 30*).

5 Check that the line B–B is a quarter of your waist measurement. Redraw with a shorter A–B length if necessary, as there is no way of tightening the waist at a later stage without spoiling the circle. (You can always get a looser waist by trimming a millimetre or two from the waistline later on.)

6 Add the length of B–C to the length A–B and put the pin through the tape measure at this point. Pin again through A and draw the curve for the hemline, C–C.

7 The pattern is for the back which has a centre-back seam for economy of fabric, so mark a straight-grain arrow. However, it is also for the front which is in one piece, so mark also a fold arrow.

8 Cut out, discarding the shaded areas shown on the diagram.

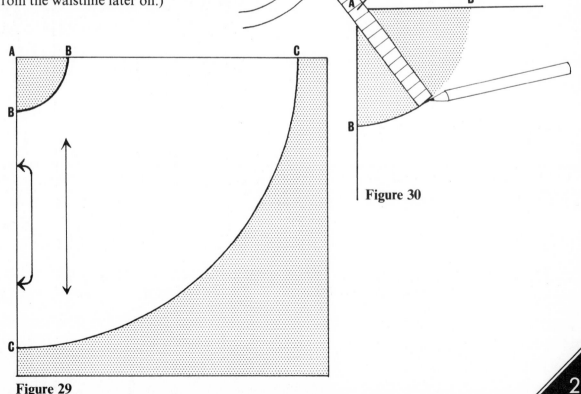

Figure 30

Figure 29

DESIGNING THE PATTERN

Low-flared skirt

You may want a skirt fitted well below the hips, but flared out at the hemline – see right-hand sketch of *Figure 23*. The yoked skirt on page 16 is another example. This design is especially useful for long skirts which can have a wide fluted hemline without taking up a vast amount of fabric.

1 Cut a six-panelled pattern (instructions on pages 14–15) with the side-front and side-back seams moved so that the centre panels are half the width of the side panels. This will give all the sections the same hem measurement, as the centre sections are cut to a fold. Add length as needed (*Figure 31*).

2 Decide the final hem width and the level from which the fullness should spring.

3 On each panel mark this level, A, on both seamlines.

4 Draw the hemline one-sixth of the new hem measurement, adding the width equally at each side, and curving up the hemline so that its length below A is the same as the original seamline (*Figure 32*).

5 Curve out the angle at A to give a smooth line, and mark a notch.

6 Mark a fold arrow on the centre panels and a straight-grain arrow down the *centre* of the side panels.

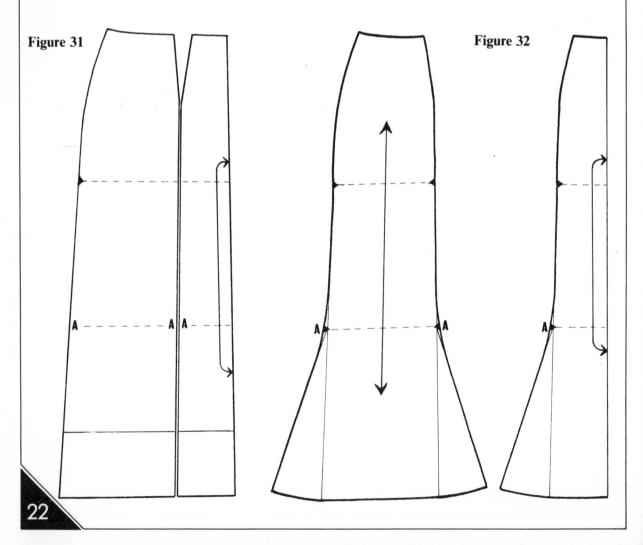

Figure 31

Figure 32

The grain line for flared skirts
Usually skirts are cut with the straight grain –
the threads parallel to the selvages – running
down the centre-back and centre-front. In
skirts with four or more panels, the
straight-grain arrow should run down the
centre of each panel. Skirts keep their shape
better when cut in this way, and jersey fabrics
should always be cut with the wale of the knit
running down the centre of the panel.

But if you want a bias-cut skirt of woven
fabric, it is quite possible to place the
centre-front and back on the true cross. This is
usually done for a fairly straight, two-, three-
or four-piece skirt, to give a softer drape.
For easier cutting out, centre panels should be
drafted whole (on folded paper) rather than
with a fold arrow (*Figure 33*).

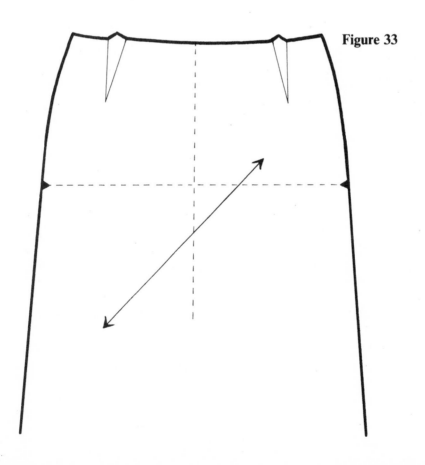

Figure 33

DESIGNING THE PATTERN

SKIRTS WITH GODETS

Godets are triangular pieces of fabric inset to give a flared or pleated effect at a skirt hem (*Figure 34*). They are most easily set into an existing seamline, and are most effective on an otherwise straight skirt.

1 Decide the length of the godet insertion, and mark a notch on the seamline.

2 Decide the hemline width of the godet – the triangle should be taller than it is wide.

3 Draft the triangle, with its sides the length of the skirt seam below the notch and its base the hemline width you have chosen. In a checked fabric, godets may look well cut on the cross to show contrast. Otherwise, mark a vertical straight-grain arrow (*Figure 35*).

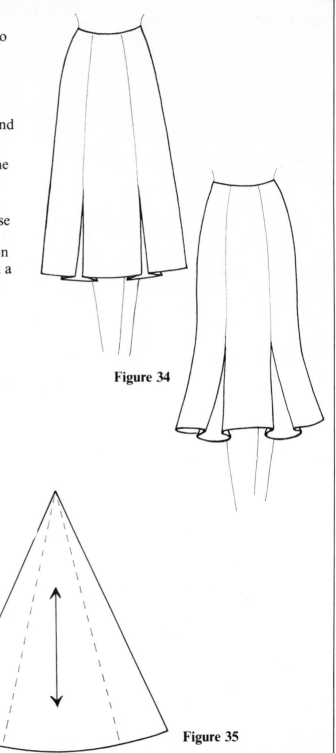

Figure 34

Figure 35

PLEATED SKIRTS

Pleats are usually – and most easily – planned on the straight grain of the fabric, between seams. But in all-round pleated skirts they may need to be shaped above the hip, and seams must be planned to come at the inner, hidden crease of the pleat. Usually, pleats are stitched part-way down.

Each pleat will take up three times its own width of fabric, so a pleated section of skirt 20 cm wide would need 60 cm of cloth – an extra 40 cm. A lot of pleats are bound to be expensive in fabric. (Sunray and concertina pleating, which are more economical, are endlessly troublesome unless the fabric is heat-set, an industrial process permanently successful only on fabrics containing man-made fibres and not possible to do with a domestic iron.)

Knife pleats

These are formed with two creases (*Figure 36*). They may be used singly as a kick-pleat, or repeated in a group, as in a kilt, without any intervening spaces (*Figure 37*).

Inverted pleats

These are formed by a pair of knife pleats, with their outer creases touching. They are most often used at the skirt centre-front or centre-back (*Figure 38*).

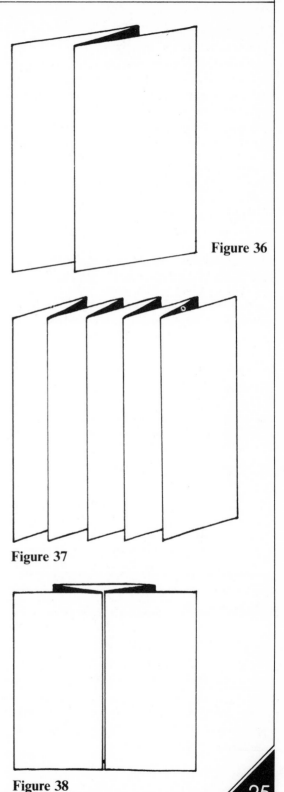

Figure 36

Figure 37

Figure 38

Box pleats

These are made by a pair of knife pleats with their outer creases pointing away from each other (*Figure 39*). Their inner creases may be planned to touch, as here, or may be spaced apart. In either case, there is a flat panel between the pleats. A box pleat may form the centre of a group of knife pleats (*Figure 40*).

Unpressed pleats

For a soft, easy shape, such as the silk-hopsack skirt on page 19 any type of pleat may be left unpressed and either stitched part-way or not at all.

Drafting pleats

The simplest possible pleating is at the centre-front or centre-back, where the pleats are on the straight grain for their full length and the position of the darts is not affected. The development of such a pattern is shown in the photograph on page 12, and the 'beginner's' skirt made from the pattern is on page 19.

1 Trace round the block.

2 Mark in the lines for the pleats. Here, one pleat will fall at the centre-front and one at each side, so only a single line is marked on the half-pattern.

3 Cut down the pleat line. Over fresh paper, spread the pattern pieces apart, keeping the cut edges parallel and the hip and hemlines level. The space between the pieces should be *double* the width you have planned for the pleat.

4 Draw round the new outline, adding the *single* width of the pleat at the centre-front fold. Mark a fold arrow.

5 Mark in the finished length of the skirt. In the photograph, seam and hem allowances have also been added; this should not be done yet. Other styling details, such as side seam pockets, may affect the final outline – the allowances are added last.

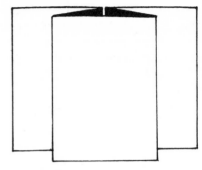

Figure 39

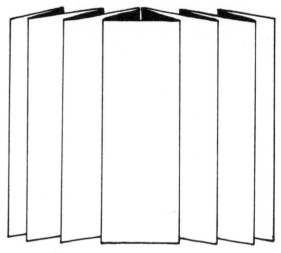

Figure 40

DESIGNING THE PATTERN

Some finished designs for pleated skirts are shown in *Figure 41*. The diagrams that follow (*Figures 42–48*) explain how the pattern for each sketch is developed.

Figure 41

DESIGNING THE PATTERN

Sketch (a): Box pleat flanked by knife pleats (pattern for this style *Figure 42*)

At the centre-front, leave half the width of the box pleat. *Add* twice the width of the pleat underlay. Leave the width of the knife pleat. *Add* twice its width.

There is no dart. Shape the top of the knife pleat markings 1 cm outwards as shown, to divide the dart width between them.

Sketch (b): Two inverted pleats (pattern for this style *Figure 43*)

At the centre-front, leave half the width between the pleats. *Add* double the pleat width. Shape the pleat markings 1 cm outwards as shown, dividing the dart width between them.

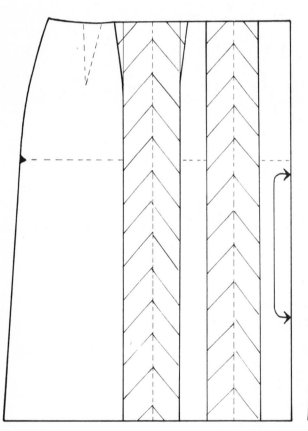

Figure 42

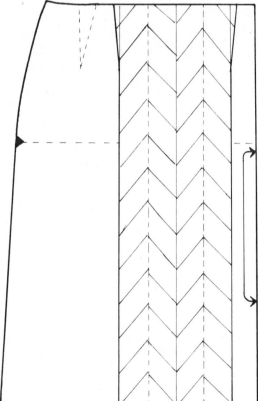

Figure 43

DESIGNING THE PATTERN

Sketch (c): Two pairs of unpressed knife pleats (pattern for this style *Figure 44*)
At the centre-front, leave half the space between the pleats. *Add* twice the width of each pleat, leaving a pleat width between. Shape both edges of both pleats 0·5 cm outwards, to compensate for the dart.

Sketch (d): All-round knife pleats (pattern for this style *Figure 45*)
Draft this skirt on a rectangle of paper, cut the finished length of the skirt by three times the hip measurement. This is not an easy pattern to make up – attempt it in a thin, firmly-woven fabric only.

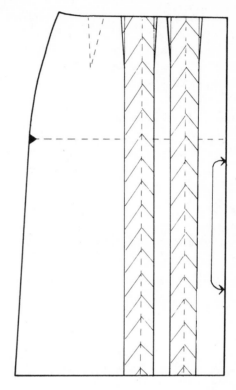

Figure 44

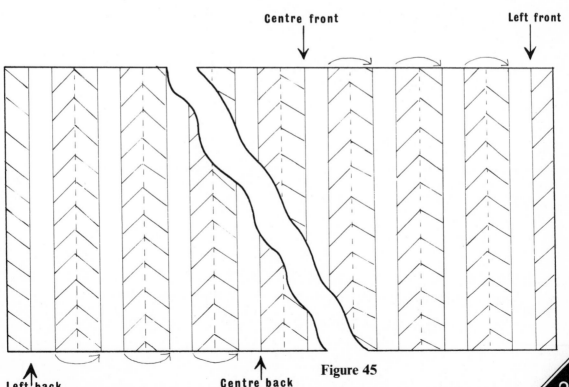

Centre front

Left front

Left back

Centre back

Figure 45

DESIGNING THE PATTERN

1 Decide the number of pleats. If you choose to have 16 pleats right round the skirt, and your hip measurement happens to be 96 cm, each pleat will be 6 cm wide and take up 18 cm of fabric. (The sum is unlikely to be as simple as this, but absolute accuracy is essential.)

2 Mark each pleat in its three sections: the front of the pleat and its two under layers. The left side opening should be at the inside crease of a pleat.

3 Mark the positions for seamlines at the inside crease of a pleat. You are likely to need more than one seam; check the width of your fabric.

4 There are no darts. The shaping between hip and waist is made on the fabric, after the seams have been stitched and the pleats tacked in place.

Sketch (e): Flared skirt with inverted centre-front pleat flanked by spaced knife pleats (pattern for this style *Figure 46*)
First draft the four-gore skirt pattern (*Figure 27*). The centre-front seam will be omitted.

1 Cut the front pattern at the lines of the knife pleats. Spread apart, adding double the width of the pleats. Make them wider at the hem than at the waist, to keep waist and hemlines as even curves.

2 Add the width of the inverted pleat at centre-front, and mark a fold arrow.

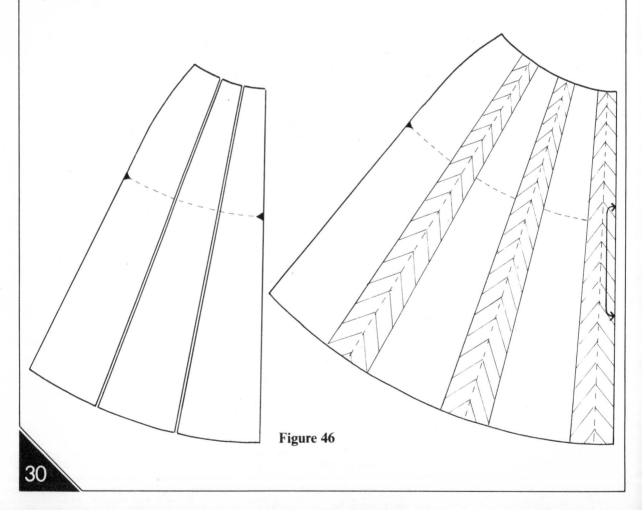

Figure 46

3 If your fabric is wide enough, you could cut the whole front in one piece. However, the skirt will hang better (and if checked, look better) if divided into panels at the inside crease of each pleat (dotted lines), with the straight grain running down the centre of the panel. The underlay of the centre inverted pleat would then be cut separately (pattern for this style *Figure 47*).

Sketch (f): Three knife pleats at one side (pattern for this style *Figure 48*)
1 Use the front block, but trace round it over a double thickness of paper, folded down the right-hand side.

2 Open out the pattern and trace the right dart only.

3 Cut and spread apart the left half of the pattern, adding double the width of each pleat.

4 Shape the top of the pleat markings as shown, dividing the dart width between them: 0·3 cm only on each seamline.

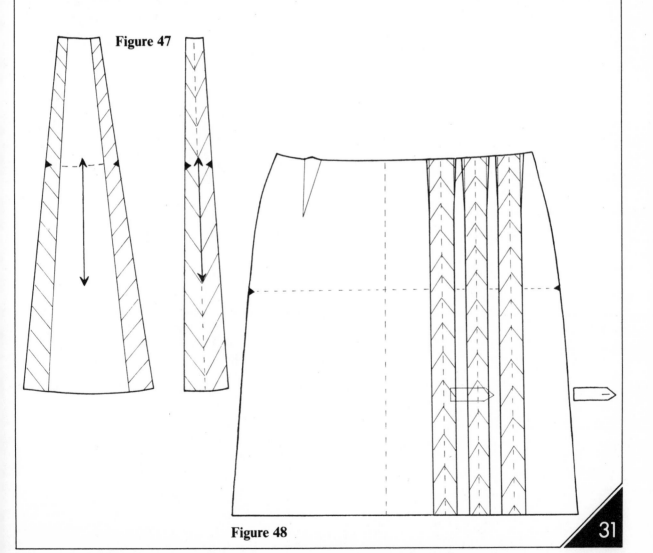

Figure 47

Figure 48

31

DESIGNING THE PATTERN

Pleats at centre-back (finished designs shown in *Figure 49*)
A fairly long, straight skirt will need some striding room. Add either an inverted pleat or a knife pleat to the existing centre-back seam.

Sketch (g): An inverted pleat should have a separate underlay, as in *Figure 47*; then only half the width of the pleat is added to the centre-back of the skirt pattern.

Sketch (h): For a knife pleat, no separate underlay is needed as the seam will fall at the inside of the pleat; add to the centre-back the single width of the pleat, not less than 5 cm.

Sketch (j): shows the use of pleats at the back of a long skirt. These may be widely flared and cut in panels as for *Sketch (e)*. They will take up a great deal of fabric, but the effect of the sweeping line could be dramatic.

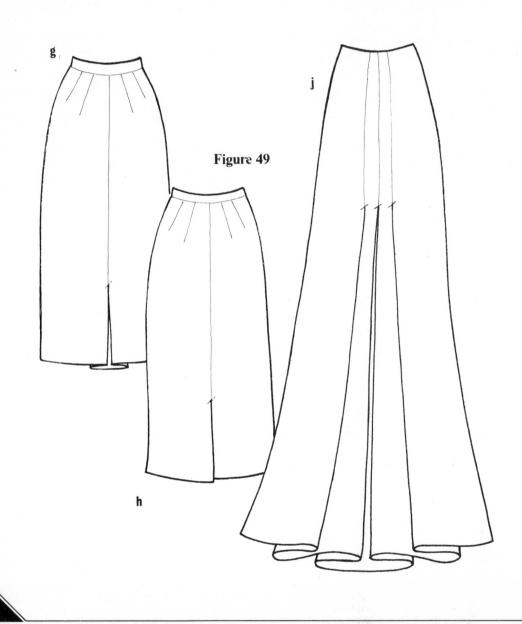

Figure 49

DESIGNING THE PATTERN

Part-way pleats (finished designs shown in *Figure 50*)

Pleats set below a yoke, or in a hemline panel, give fullness and movement to the skirt without bulk at the waist. They also need less fabric.

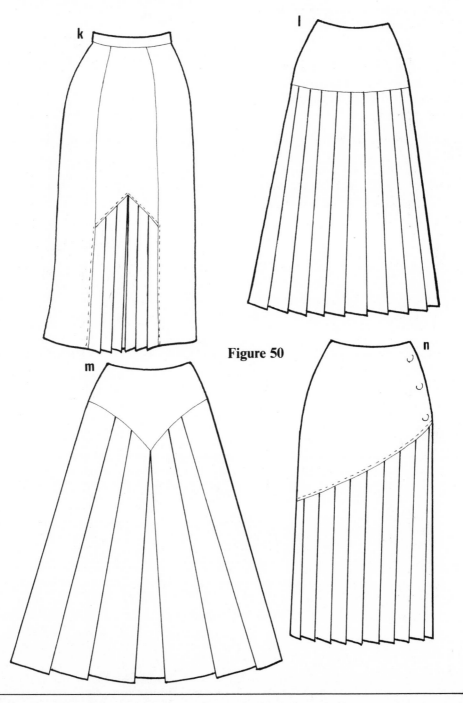

Figure 50

Sketch (k): Inset panel of pleats
1 Cut the skirt to the six-panelled pattern
(*Figure 16*).

2 On the centre-front panel, draw in the shape
of the inset and cut it away.

3 Pleat a length of paper into knife pleats or,
as here, an inverted pleat flanked by pairs of
knife pleats.

4 Centre the pleated paper under the prepared
skirt panel and draw round the dotted
seamline (*Figure 51*). Cut along the line and
unfold the inset pattern.

Sketch (l): Pleats from a straight hip yoke
Pleats from the hipline are easier to make up
than those from the waistline because no
shaping is needed. Cut the yoke as shown in
Figures 20–22. Draft the skirt on a rectangle
of paper as in *Figure 45*.

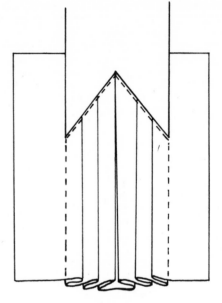

Figure 51

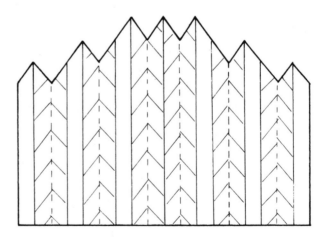

Sketch (m): Knife pleats from a shaped yoke
1 Use the four-gore pattern and draft the whole skirt front in the same way as for *Sketch (e)* in *Figure 41* and as shown in *Figure 46*.

2 Fold in the pleats and draw across them the seamline for the yoke. Cut along this line.

3 Unfold the skirt pattern. The upper ends of the pleats will then be correctly shaped (*Figure 52*).

4 Fold in the pleats across the yoke and trace round, for the yoke pattern. Mark notches to correspond to the pleats.

Sketch (n): Knife pleats from a shaped seamline
1 Pleat a length of paper as in *Figure 45*. The depth should be the measurement from hip to hemline.

2 Using the front block, cut a pattern from paper folded down the right-hand side. Unfold so that you have a whole pattern.

3 Mark the diagonal seamline across it, sloping downwards from the left hip-level notch. Cut along this line and discard the lower section.

4 Place the upper section over the pleated paper. Draw and cut along the seamline. Unfold the pleated section (*Figure 53*).

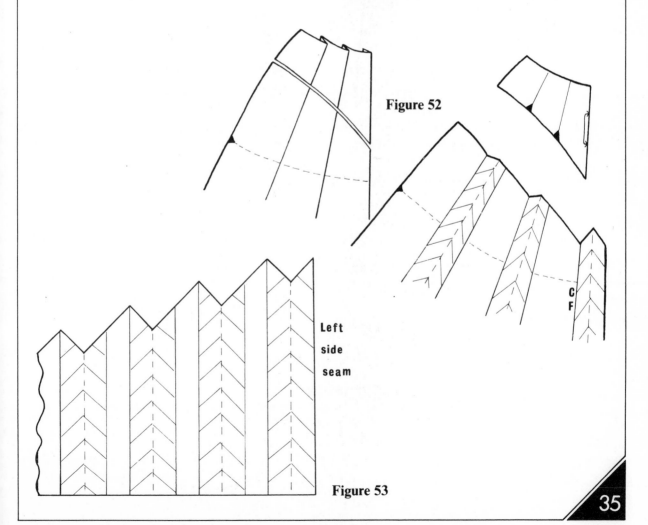

Figure 52

Left side seam

C F

Figure 53

35

GATHERED SKIRTS (*Figure 54*)
The effectiveness of gathering in a skirt depends just as much on the material as on the pattern. Sheer fabrics, fine silky jerseys or fine crêpes are ideal. Their lightness allows one to set up to half as much again into the seamline, and their suppleness shows off the graceful movement that gathers can give.

A small amount of gathering can look well on thin woollen fabrics; it is surprising how little extra will give a gathered effect, and the temptation is always to use too much. The unattractive bunchy look of many summer skirts is the result of exuberantly lavish gathering on an unsympathetic fabric. You might sometimes want a totally unshaped dirndl style, as in the lowest sketch; but if you did, the pattern would be a rectangle. It could be successful in a voile.

For dress cottons, moderate gatherings set into a fitted yoke will hang better and look more controlled. Extra hem width can always be added by flaring the skirt panels.

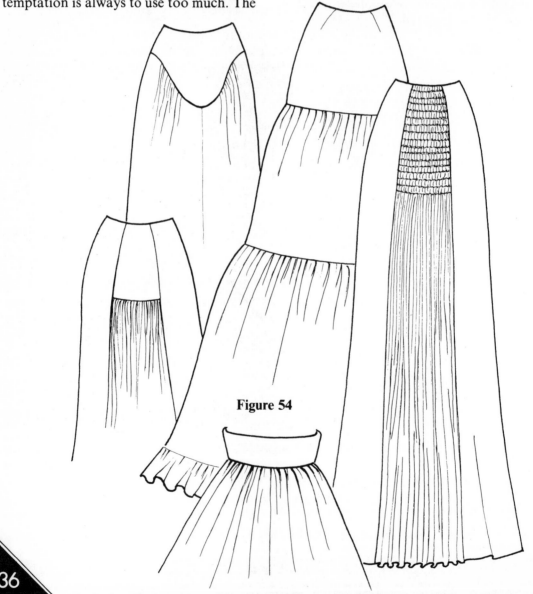

Figure 54

DESIGNING THE PATTERN

The top left-hand sketch shows a shaped yoke – the same design as the fine polyester jersey skirt on this page, where only 5 cm each side of the yoke was added for the gathers. The four-gore pattern should be used (*Figure 27*), adapted as in *Figure 55*.

Gathers in tiers, as in the centre sketch, are a good way of obtaining hem fullness while retaining some fit at waist and hip. Tiers are also more economical in fabric. They should be graduated, becoming deeper as they go down. The hip section should be cut directly from the block. The other skirt sections are rectangles, the bottom one as wide as you want the hemline to be, and the centre one midway between the hem and hip measurements.

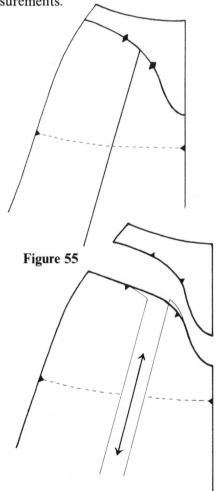

Figure 55

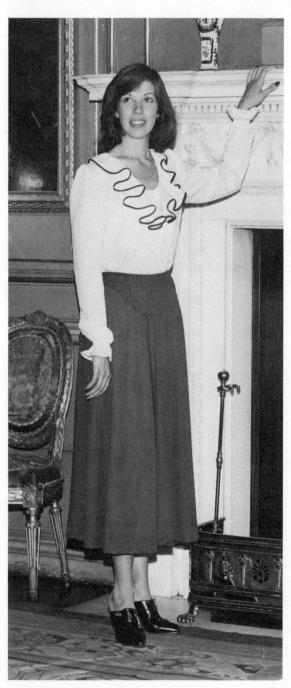

Yoked and gathered skirt in polyester jersey

37

DESIGNING THE PATTERN

A hemline flounce or frill can finish this type of skirt. The frill can be cut on the cross for a softer line, and could be folded double, with both raw edges included in the hem seam – a quick finish that saves working a long hem. It should be cut as a straight strip. A flounce would normally be cut as a segment of a circle – *Figure 56* – the shorter edge being gathered to the skirt, or set on without gathering. Flounces tend to take up an inordinate amount of fabric, but can be very graceful at a shaped hemline, as in *Figure 57*.

The centre-left sketch shows how a gathered section can form part of the centre panel of a six-piece skirt. Draft the skirt as in *Figures 16* and *17,* and adapt the pattern as shown in *Figure 58.* A similar skirt, the long one in the right-hand sketch, has the centre panel cut wider for its full length, the top section being shirred. This looks particularly well, as here, at the back of a skirt.

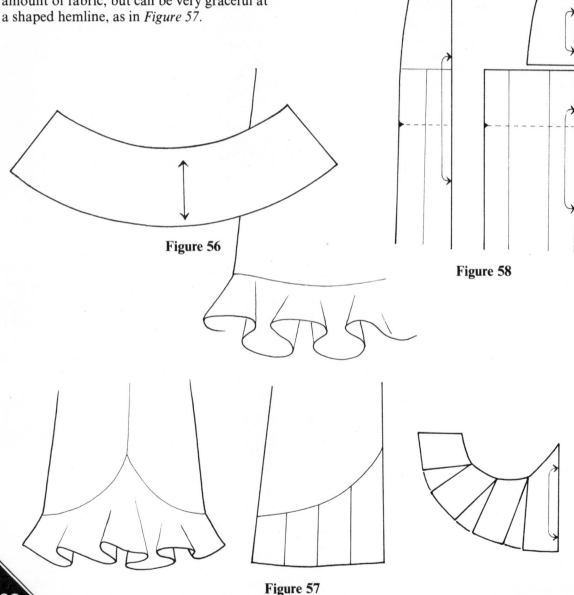

Figure 56

Figure 58

Figure 57

DRAPED SKIRTS (*Figure 59*)

Once you become enthusiastic about draping, it can be as compulsive as patchwork and you may find yourself draping everything. Drafting the patterns is straightforward, but the difficulty lies in deciding the proportions and the quantity of fullness. A good eye is much more important than a tape measure.

Any really elaborate drapery should be modelled in muslin directly on a dress-form, and the pattern taken from the muslin. However, the simple draping that one might use in a design for a skirt can be worked out quite satisfactorily on paper from the outset. Small adjustments to the tacked-up skirt can later be made on the figure.

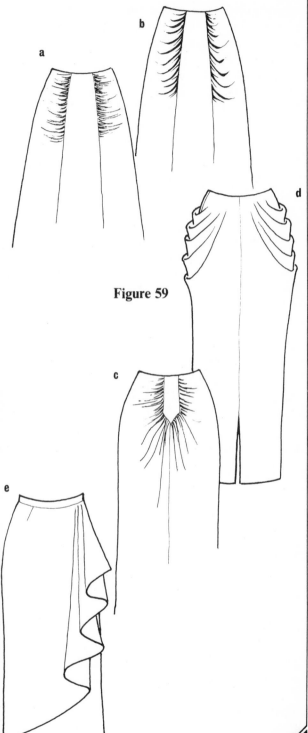

Figure 59

Wrapover skirt in gaberdine

Sketch (a): The simplest form of draping, yet a very effective one, is the setting of gathers into a vertical seam. The six-piece skirt pattern (*Figure 16*) is altered by cutting the side-front into strips as shown in *Figure 60*, and spreading the strips apart at their inner ends. This extra length forms horizontal draping but leaves a clean line at the side seam.

Sketch (b): If you want the draping to fall in folds, then extra width as well as extra length needs to be added to the draped panel. The more you add, the deeper the drape. Try pinning the fabric to the skirt you are wearing, to judge how much depth you want in the draped section. It could be as little as 5 cm. Add this width as shown in *Figure 61*. In order to hold the seamlines in place, and preserve the looseness of the draped panel, it will need to be backed by a lining cut to the regular skirt pattern.

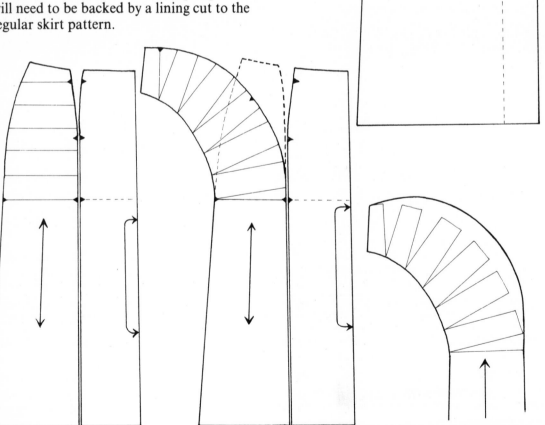

Figure 62

Figure 60

Figure 61

Sketch (c): A variation of the previous styles, using the front pattern block (*Figure 12*). Here, the draping is caught into a centre-front strap, as shown in *Figure 62*.

Sketch (d): This skirt should be made in a fine, soft fabric if the hip drapes are to hang gracefully. There is no side seam below the draped section and as the skirt will have a very narrow hemline it will need a centre-front slit. The rather startling pattern is cut as follows:

1 Trace round the back and front blocks and cut out. Trim down the side seams so that the width at hem and hip is the same (*Figure 63*).

2 Cut out the dart markings and slash the patterns as shown. The actual shape of the cuts does not matter, but they should not be within 7 cm of the centre-front or back.

3 Sellotape together two lengths of drafting paper, as shown on *Figure 64* by the dotted line. Make sure the top edge of the paper is at right angles to the sellotaped join.

4 Spread out the sections of back and front so that the top section of each side seam lies along the top of the paper. The sections must touch at their waistline edges. Arrange the lower ends of the side seams to touch, on the centre line.

A–B is the centre-back.
C–D is the centre-front.
B–D is the hemline, which should be curved off.
A–E is the back waistline, which should be a smooth curve.
C–F is the front waistline, also smoothly curved.
E–G and F–G are the edges of the short side seam, which will drop inside the draping. (The shorter you make this seam, the higher the draping will hang; a higher line will look more elegant.)

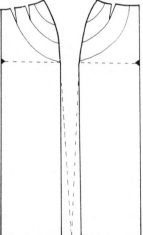

Figure 63

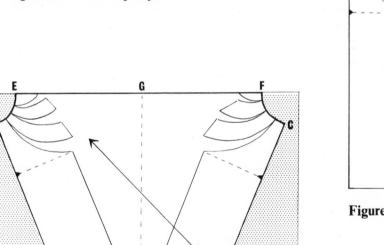

Figure 64

DESIGNING THE PATTERN

5 Mark a straight-grain arrow diagonally across the pattern. Cut out, discarding the shaded area.

Sketch (e): Free-hanging drapery can be used on either a firm or a soft fabric; a stiff taffeta, say, would give a dramatically different effect from a crêpe. Note that this is a three-piece skirt. The right side-seam will take in the edges of both the overskirt and the underskirt.

1 Cut the back and front patterns from the unaltered blocks.

2 For the overskirt, mark the waistline A–B, the right side seam and the hemline. Fold in the left dart (*Figure 65*). Draw in the line you want for the draped edge C–D and measure the length of this line.

3 Measure the length B–C and draw it horizontally from B to E.

4 Draw a curve from D to E. Check its length with D–C. If D–E is shorter, move E upwards, to lengthen the curve; but if D–E is longer, drop E a little way down the curve.

5 Cut the pattern along the final lines of A–B–E–D. Mark a straight-grain arrow. Mark a notch at B.

6 The reverse of the draped panel will show, so you will need to cut a facing – either from matching or contrasting fabric. (Think of the impact of a black evening skirt faced with white or a brilliant colour.) The dotted line B–F shows the inner edge; trace the facing from the shape B–E–F and mark the same straight-grain line as for the overskirt.

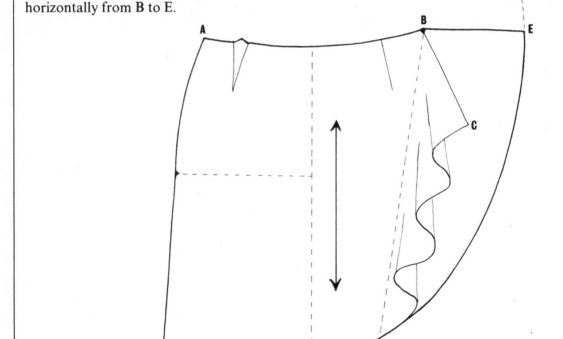

Figure 65

WRAPOVER SKIRTS

The straight skirt on page 39 has a wrapover reaching to within 5 cm of the side seam. A pleated or front-buttoned style need not have such a wide wrap, but it should still be generous enough to prevent the skirt from falling open when you sit down.

1 Draft the back and front patterns. The back can be pleated or flared, but there should be no fullness at the centre-front. Cut the front pattern whole, on paper folded down the right-hand side.

2 On the front pattern, draw in the line you want for the overskirt. Use this pattern for both fronts (*Figure 66*).

3 Cut a facing 7 cm wide (as shown by the thin line), shaped to match the front edges. (If the wrapover is straight, the facing is simply an extension of the front edge.)

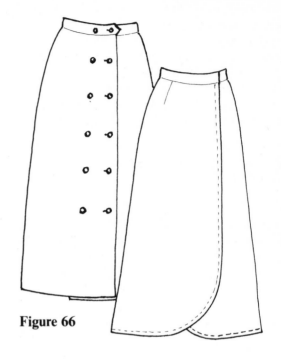

Figure 66

Kilts

A kilt can have a narrower overlap, held in place with a kilt-pin. Draft the pattern as for the all-round knife-pleated skirt in *Figure 45*. The overlap and underlap, each 20–22 cm wide, are not pleated (*Figure 67*).

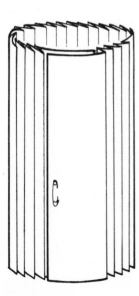

Figure 67

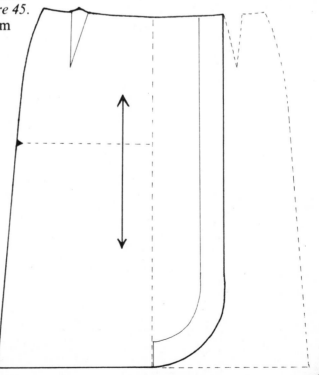

POCKETS (*Figure 68*)

The kinds of pocket, their placing and their proportion are of great importance to the design, as they are so conspicuous. It is, as always, easier to judge the effect on the figure than on paper, so chalk the line for a bound pocket, or the shape of a patch pocket, on an existing skirt. When you are satisfied, transfer the markings to the skirt front pattern.

Seam allowances are included in the following patterns, where the pocket is cut separately from the garment.

Sketch (a): Seamline pocket

This unobtrusive pocket (shown in the skirt on page 19) can be cut in one with the skirt back and front (*Figure 69*). If the fabric is thick, the pocket front should be cut separately, in lining material, and seamed to the skirt. Do not make the pocket opening longer than necessary, or it may gape. The pocket bag should be half as deep again as the opening, and 13 cm wide. Draw a rectangle at the side of the skirt to help you shape the pocket as shown. Seam allowances are added when the skirt pattern is complete.

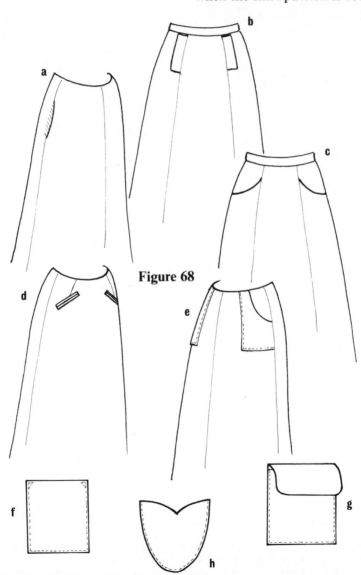

Figure 68

DESIGNING THE PATTERN

Sketch (b): Welted pocket
This is best set in the side-front seam. It is cut in the same way as the previous pocket, but the pocket front must be cut as a separate piece. Draft the welt so that it is twice its finished width and the same length as the opening; add to it seam allowances of 1·5 cm all round (*Figure 70*).

Sketch (c): Panel pocket
This is set between the side and side-front seams. Cut the patterns as shown in *Figure 71*, adding seam allowances of 1·5 cm. The side-front skirt panel is cropped to form the pocket mouth.

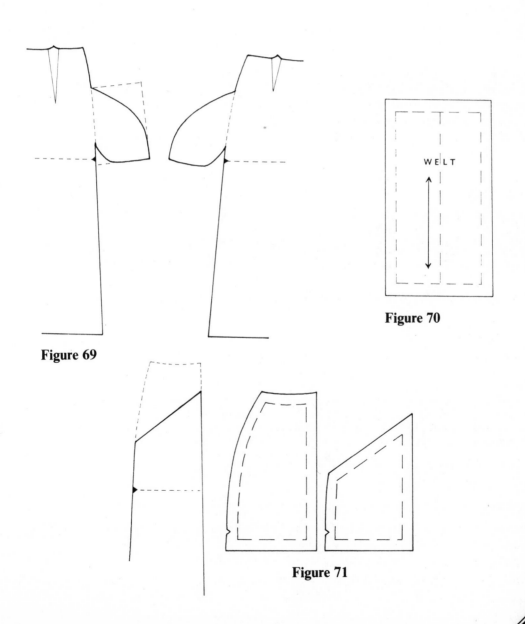

WELT

Figure 69

Figure 70

Figure 71

DESIGNING THE PATTERN

Sketch (d): Bound pocket
These pockets need accurate workmanship and are rather more difficult to make than the previous types.

1 Draw the line of the pocket mouth on the skirt pattern (*Figure 72*). It should be wide enough for your hand, plus 2 cm; 10 cm should be enough. Above and below the opening, draw the width of the binding: about 0·6–0·8 cm.

2 Below the pocket draw in the depth of the pocket bag.

3 Draft the pocket as in *Figure 73:*
Twice the depth of the pocket bag, plus
Six times the depth of the binding, plus
3 cm for seam allowances – say a total of 25 cm
The *width* is the width of the pocket mouth, plus 3 cm.

4 Mark a straight-grain arrow diagonally across the pocket.

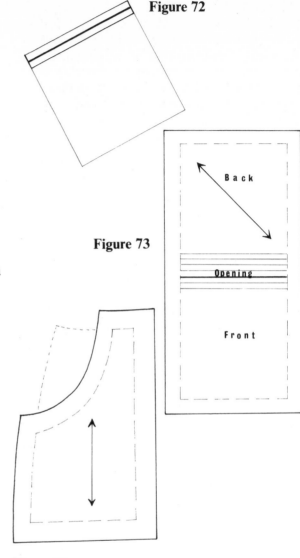

Figure 72

Figure 73

Sketch (e): Patch pocket from side seam
This type of pocket – very simple to apply – has two edges top-stitched to the skirt front. The top edge is taken into the waist finish, and the remaining edge taken into the side seam.

Mark the outline on the skirt front pattern. Trace the shape from the pattern, add 1·5 cm seam allowances all round and cut out. The pocket lining is cut to the same pattern (*Figure 74*).

Figure 74

Sketch (f): Patch pocket
Plain rectangular patch pockets are the easiest of all to set on.

1 Draw the finished shape of the pocket.

2 Add 3 cm allowance at the top edge, for the facing and seam. Add 1·5 cm along the other edges (*Figure 75*).

3 For the lining, add nothing to the top edge, but 1·5 cm along the others. The lining seam will fall 1·5 cm inside the pocket opening.

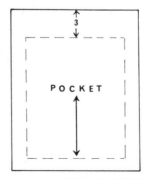

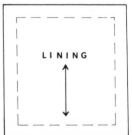

Figure 75

Sketch (g): Patch pocket with a flap
Add twice the depth of the flap to the length of the pocket; then add 3 cm for the facing and seam allowance. Add 1·5 cm along the other edges. The lining is cut as above for a plain patch pocket (*Figure 76*).

Sketch (h): Patch pocket with a shaped opening
Where the pocket mouth is not cut straight, a seam will be needed along the opening. Pocket and lining are therefore drafted to the finished size, both with 1·5 cm seam allowances added all round.

THE OPENING AND WAIST FINISH

Zip
Most skirts will be closed with a side or back zip (US zipper). No alteration is needed to the pattern unless you want a concealed zip with a shield behind it, at side or centre-front. See the right and wrong side photographs on page 48. In that case, add an extension 4 cm wide by 18 cm long to both skirt sections from the waistline downwards (*Figure 77*).

There are three ways to finish a skirt waist; with petersham ribbon (US grosgrain ribbon), with a waistband, or with waistline facings. There is no alteration to the skirt pattern for any of these.

Waistband
The simplest kind, a narrow band up to 5 cm wide, can be cut straight. It should be the length of the skirt waist plus 3 cm for an underlap if needed. Draft it double the finished width, and mark on it notches to correspond to the positions of the skirt seams (*Figure 78*).

Waistbands wider than 5 cm, as in the lowest sketch of Figure 54, should be shaped to the waist. If the lower edge of a deep band is to be set on the natural waistline, its upper edge will have to be lengthened.

1 Cut a strip of paper the length and width you want the band to be. Mark notches to correspond to the skirt seams.

2 Slash the pattern at and between each notch, as shown in *Figure 79*, and spread apart 0·4 cm at each slash – making a total of a scant 3 cm extra length.

3 A shaped band will have a seam at its top edge, so cut an identical facing.

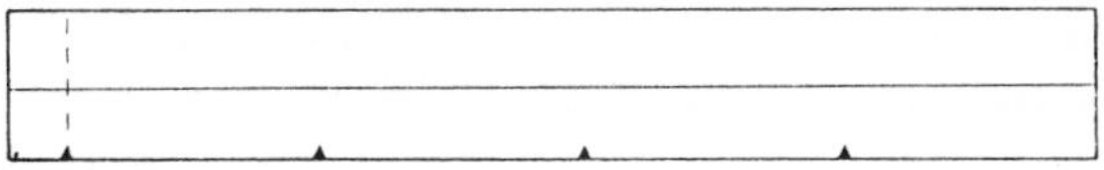

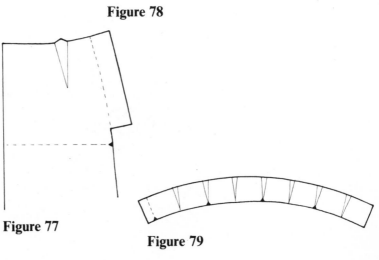

Figure 78

Figure 79

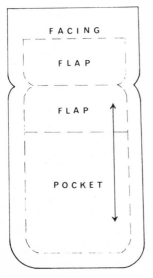

Figure 76

Figure 77

Waistline Facings

For a lightweight skirt, such as the jersey one on page 16, waistline facings make a firm enough finish. They would not do for a heavy tweed, or for a lined skirt. Trace them, 7 cm deep or more, from the tops of the skirt sections. Fold out the darts to obtain the final shape of the facing (*Figure 80*).

The facings for a yoked skirt should be cut from the yoke patterns.

THE LINING

Linings are normally cut to the same pattern as the skirt, shortened 5 cm at the hemline.

There would be little purpose in lining a fully pleated skirt, but if you want a lining it should be cut short, just below the length to which the pleats are stitched down.

Wrapover skirts are not lined.

SEAM AND HEM ALLOWANCES

The patterns have been drafted 'net' without any turnings. The edges of the pattern pieces all coincide with seamlines or with the length of a finished edge. Now, with all the pieces drafted, is the time to add seam and hem allowances, as in the photograph on page 12.

1 Add 1·5 cm seam allowances to all seamlines, including:
the waist edges and waistband;
the edges of pockets cut in one with skirt sections;
the edges of any zip extension;
the edges of any yoke, godet, frill, flounce or facing.

2 For a very flared hemline, add a 2 cm hem allowance. A wider hem would not set well.

3 For sheer fabrics cut on the straight grain, add 16 cm at the hemline. This would be turned up in two lays each of 8 cm, to give weight to the hemline.

4 For all other hemlines, add 5 cm.

Nothing is added to edges marked with a fold arrow.

Draw or rule at these distances outside all the pattern outlines, and cut out. Cut notches along the new edges. Check that the names of the pieces, and straight-grain lines or fold arrows, are marked on all of them.

These are the final patterns, ready for laying out on the fabric.

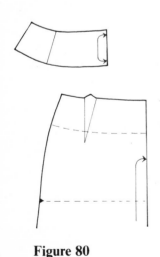

Figure 80

48

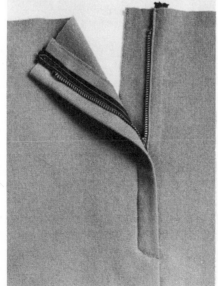

Concealed zip setting: right side

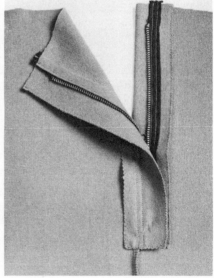

Concealed zip setting: wrong side

DESIGNING THE PATTERN

FABRIC REQUIREMENTS

As you are not working with a commercial pattern you will not have the guidance, given on the pattern envelope, as to the length of fabric needed.

So first choose your fabric, note its width and also any check or surface texture that may have to be matched. Next, make a pattern layout to see how much you will need to buy. Only then, buy the fabric.

The pattern layout

Unless you have a really large table, plan the layout of the pattern pieces on the floor.

1 Take the width of the fabric when folded in half, with the selvages matched. Use the edge of a carpet to represent the fold of the fabric, and a long ruler or straight edge, placed parallel to it and the appropriate distance away, to represent the selvage edges.

2 Place your pattern pieces, as economically as possible, with straight-grain arrows parallel to the edges and fold arrows on the fold. *Figure 81* shows a typical skirt layout. A wide skirt may need to be pieced as shown.

3 Check the number of pattern pieces you will need. As your fabric will be folded, you will automatically cut two of each piece. But you may need four pieces for lined patch pockets, so patterns for these will have to be cut twice over.

4 If you have chosen a napped fabric – such as corduroy – with a one-way surface texture, or a material with a one-way design, then all the pattern pieces must be laid with their tops towards the same end of the layout. An uneven check, such as the one in *Figure 82*, must be treated in the same way.

5 For a checked fabric, or one with a large design, add one complete repeat of the fabric pattern to the measured length of your layout, to allow for precise matching.

6 For a circular or very fully flared skirt, measure your layout as if on the full width of the fabric, imagining a selvage at each side of the layout and a fold across the end – so that you will still be planning your layout on a double thickness.

The fabric and notions

Only now are you ready to calculate the length needed, and to buy the fabric and lining. At the same time, buy what Americans call the 'notions' – the necessary bits and pieces to make up the skirt:
18 cm zip;
matching thread and if necessary buttonhole twist for top-stitching;
waistline hook and bar;
seam binding or bias binding for hems;
a strip of interfacing for the waistband and pocket welts – heavy iron-on Vilene is suitable,
or lighter-weight interfacing for waistline facings,
or petersham ribbon, 2·5 cm wide;
tape for reinforcing waistline facings.

Figure 81

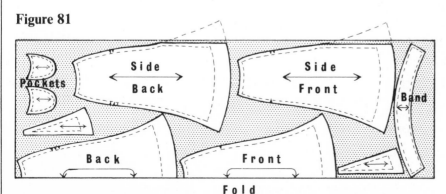

Figure 82

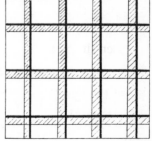

MAKING UP THE SKIRT

The instructions that follow give the order in which you should work, whatever type of skirt you are making. As you go along, pick out the instructions for your particular design and disregard the rest.

CUTTING OUT
Fold the fabric lengthwise, with the right side inside. It is important that the selvages (or stripes of a patterned fabric) should be perfectly matched, so that the fold is exactly on the straight grain of the fabric.

Place the pattern pieces in the positions you have planned, with their straight-grain lines parallel to the selvages and the fold arrows precisely to the fold, not a millimetre or two away from it. With a checked material, plan the most conspicuous line – or the centre of the space between – to run down the centre-front and centre-back.

Smooth the pieces down their centres, hold them with one pin at each end, check the straight-grain arrow again, and then smooth out and pin down the corners. Finally, pin all round the edges at intervals of 10–15 cm.

Cut out. When you come to a notch, cut outwards, not into the seam allowance; you might need that width to let out a seam.

Leave the patterns pinned to the skirt pieces.

MARKING
The patterns already have their seam allowances marked round the fitting lines. It is important that your seams are stitched precisely along these lines, or the fit will be affected. So mark the vital points, through the pattern on to the fabric, as a guide for machining. There are several ways to do this.

Dressmaker's carbon paper
Insert the carbon paper (face downwards) between the pattern and the upper layer of fabric; place another carbon (face upwards) under the lower layer. On a firm surface, mark through the pattern with the tracing wheel, making a cross at the point to be marked. The marks will be transferred to the wrong side of the fabric.

Tailor's tacks
This method is nearly as quick, and rather more reliable, since carbon markings may not show up well on rough-surfaced fabrics.

1 Using double thread, take a tiny stitch through the pattern and both thicknesses of fabric, at the point to be marked (*Figure 83*).

2 Take another stitch through the same point, and leave a loop big enough to put your finger through (*Figure 84*).

3 Cut the thread, leaving 1 cm ends (*Figure 85*).

4 When you have marked all the points on the pattern piece, gently tear off the pattern. If your stitches were small, so will the holes be. Then ease apart the two layers of fabric, and cut the loops of thread between them (*Figure 86*).

5 You will be left with tufts of thread in each piece of fabric which can be matched with their opposite numbers when you pin the seams.

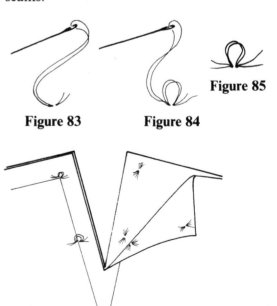

Figure 83   **Figure 84**   **Figure 85**

Figure 86

MAKING UP THE SKIRT

Points to be marked

1 The points where seamlines cross, such as the waistline ends of the skirt seams.

2 Dart markings, at the waistline and at the point.

3 Pleat markings, at the waistline or yoke, at the point to which they will be stitched, and at several points down their length. This is tedious, but essential; it is vital that pleat lines be accurately marked. It helps to mark the outer fold line, the inner fold line and the placement line in differently coloured threads. Or the lines can be chalked in and then marked with a line of tacking.

4 The level of the end-stop of the zip, measuring the opening length of the zip down from the waist fitting line.

5 The corners of pocket placings.

BEFORE FITTING

Some sections of the skirt can be permanently stitched at this stage as they will not be affected by fitting. For instance, yokes should be set on; a panel from which gathers or pleats spring should be made up now.

Gathers

1 Stitch any seam running down the centre of a gathered section.

2 Along the edge to be gathered run two gathering threads (longest machine stitch),

one of them 1 cm and the other 2 cm from the edge. Pull up to fit the yoke or panel into which the gathers are to be set (*Figure 87*).

3 With right sides together, stitch the seam. Where you have an angled seam, as in *Figure 59(c)*, work with the gathers uppermost. If necessary, clip the turnings at the corners (*Figure 88*).

Draped panels
Where a draped section needs a lining to hold its shape, as in *Figure 59(b)*, attach the lining as follows.

1 Gather the edge of the draped panel.

2 Tack the draped panel along both its edges to the lining.

3 Stitch the seam, to include both the draped section and the lining.

Shirring (as for the panel in *Figure 54*)
1 Wind the machine bobbin with elastic thread; adjust the tension if necessary, following your machine instruction booklet. Set the longest stitch.

2 Working with the right side uppermost, stitch evenly-spaced rows of shirring about 1·5 cm apart.

3 On the wrong side, pull up and tie off the ends of the elastic thread, to give the width you want for the panel.

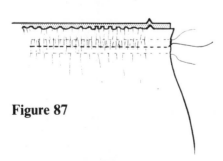

Figure 87

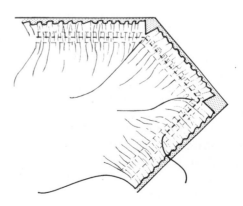

Figure 88

Tacking pleats

1 Tack all pleats for their whole length. This is easiest if you first press and tack the outer fold (*Figure 89*).

2 Then bring these folds over to their placement lines, and tack again, through all three thicknesses (*Figure 90*).

3 In an all-round pleated skirt as in *Figure 41(d)*, this second tacking goes only as far up as the hipline; later, between hip and waist, the folds will be eased together so that the pleats fit the waist.

Stitching pleats

Most pleats are stitched down for part of their length. Except for the all-round pleats above, they should be stitched now, ending with machine backstitching for strength.

In *Figure 41*, sketches (*a*) and (*f*) show top-stitched pleats, stitched from the right side. A long machine stitch with buttonhole twist makes a good, bold line.

In sketches (*b*), (*c*) and (*e*), the stitching is from the wrong side, so it does not show. Either method can be used for these pleat-seams, according to the effect you want. They can be finished with arrowheads, as in *Figure 135*.

Pleated sections below yokes or panels

Pleated sections such as those in *Figure 50* should now be set permanently into their yoke or panel. For a straight seam, place right sides together in the usual way, and stitch. For an angled seam, it may be more effective and will be easier to top-stitch.

First, press under the seam turnings of the panel or yoke, clipping any corners as necessary (*Figure 91*). Lay the panel over the pleated section, tack and top-stitch.

Godets

Godets are usually set into side-front and side-back seams, so stitch these seams down to the notch you marked for the point of the godet.

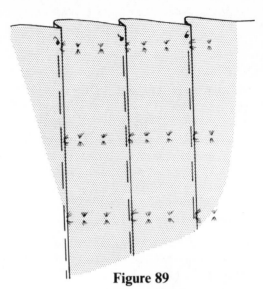

Figure 89

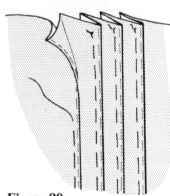

Figure 90

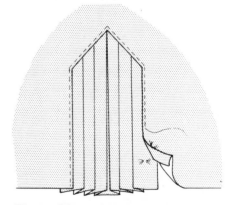

Figure 91

MAKING UP THE SKIRT

Match one edge of the godet to its skirt edge from the point down to the hemline. With the skirt side uppermost, stitch from the notch downwards.

Again from the notch downwards, stitch the other edge of the godet (*Figure 92*). Clip the seam turnings of the skirt so that they lie flat at the point of the godet.

Pockets stitched into seams
Those pockets that are stitched into a seam – *Figure 68* (*b*), (*c*) and (*e*) – should be made up next.

Sketch (*b*): *Welted pocket*
1 Press interfacing to half of welt, up to fold.

2 With right sides together, stitch the short seams at the ends *Figure 93*. Trim the turnings, turn right-side-out and press.

3 With right sides together, tack the welt to the side of the skirt *front* section, over the pocket markings.

4 Tack the front pocket piece over this, right side down. Stitch through all thicknesses along the side-front seamline. Do not stitch into the seam allowance at the ends of the pocket piece (*Figure 94*).

5 If not already cut in one with the skirt side-front, seam the back pocket piece to the side-front of the skirt.

6 Press the pocket pieces – but not the welt – outwards from the skirt sections.

7 Stitch the side-front seams, including the pocket bag, pivoting at each corner (*Figure 95*).

8 Clip the turnings so that the seam can be pressed open and the welt pressed to the side. The pocket is pressed towards the front.

9 From the wrong side of the skirt, back-stitch through to the ends of the welt, to hold it in place on the side-front.

Sketch (*c*): *Panel pocket*
1 With right sides together, stitch the bottom seam of the pocket; you will be stitching the top of the skirt side-front to the pocket front lining (*Figure 96*).

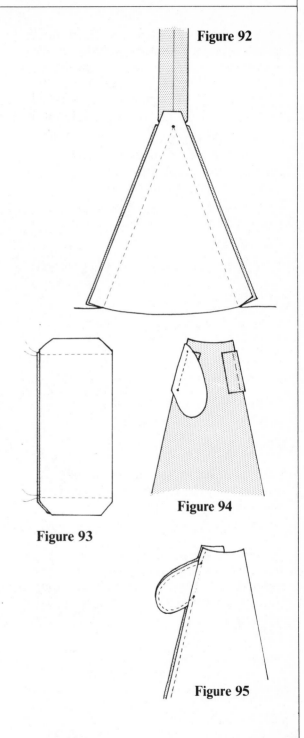

Figure 92

Figure 93

Figure 94

Figure 95

2 With right sides together, stitch the pocket mouth; you will be stitching the top of the pocket front lining to the top of the lower skirt section. Clip the turnings, turn right-side-out and press (*Figure 97*). Understitch turnings to the lining, inside pocket mouth.

3 Tack both sides of the pocket through all three thicknesses. You are now ready to stitch the whole side-front seam, but not yet the side seam which may be altered in fitting.

Sketch (e): Patch pocket from side seam
1 With right sides of pocket and lining together, stitch the pocket mouth seam.

2 Stitch the angled seam from the pocket waistline to the corner and on to the side edges (*Figure 98*).

3 Clip and trim the turnings, turn right-side-out through the side edges and press.

4 Tack in place on the skirt, matching waistline and side seam edges.

5 Top-stitch in place with buttonhole twist and a long machine stitch.

The seams
Next, permanently stitch all seams *except* the side seams, which may need to be altered during fitting. Leave open the zip placing, if it is not in a side seam.

Press seams open, unless they include pleats.

If the skirt is to be lined, there is no need to finish the raw edge of the seam turnings. For unlined skirts, work zigzag machine stitching over each edge separately. In thin fabrics only, the edges can be pressed open, folded under and stitched close to the fold.

Yokes
Set on back and front yokes next, as described above for yokes set over pleats.

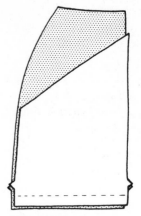

Figure 96

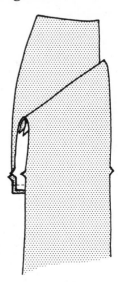

Figure 97

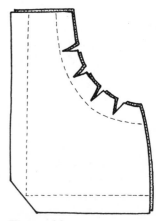

Figure 98

Tacking for fitting

Tack the darts; if their length needs to be altered, this should be done during fitting.

Tack the side seams, leaving the opening for the zip. Fitting is simpler if the side seams are tacked from the right side, with the front edge folded under and then lapped over the back edge (*Figure 99*). For the draped skirt in *Figure 59(d)*, the tacked side-seams will fall inside the hip fullness. For the skirt in *Figure 59(e)*, the right side-seam will take in the edges of both the underskirt and the draped overskirt.

Temporary waistband

Before you can fit the skirt, it should be mounted on a length of petersham as a temporary waistband. Pin the waist fitting line (1·5 cm below the raw edge) to the lower edge of the petersham.

In an all-round pleated skirt, ease in the pleats to fit the waistband measurement; they can be adjusted on the figure (*Figure 100*).

FITTING

Try on the skirt and pin together the ends of the temporary waistband. Get a friend to fit you while you stand straight.

1 Check that the skirt hangs straight down the centre-front and centre-back. If one of your hips is slightly higher than the other (quite usual), the skirt may hang towards that side. Set the skirt lower on the waistband at that side to correct the balance.

2 From the side, check that the skirt hangs vertically. If the side seam slopes forward, pin the back of the skirt slightly higher on the waistband. If the side seam hangs towards the back, raise the front of the skirt on the waistband. Very small adjustments will make all the difference to the pitch of the skirt.

3 Check the level (not the length) of the hemline. If the skirt edge hangs unevenly, mark all round with chalk a level that corresponds to the shortest part. Do not try to straighten the hem by making any alteration at waist level; that would only throw the skirt out of line. Once you have marked the level, you can decide hem depth.

4 For all-round pleated skirts, check and adjust the evenness of the pleats at the waistline. Between the waist and hip, pin each pleat in place to make a smooth line.

5 For all other skirts – those with side seams – check the curve over the hip. This is a very individual shape; the seam may need to be adjusted fractionally for a perfect line.

6 Check the length and width of the darts. They should not need altering at waist level. Lengthen a dart if there seems to be too much fabric bubbling at the dart point; shorten it if it appears to pull at the point.

7 Mark any alterations clearly with chalk, tailor's tacks or pins.

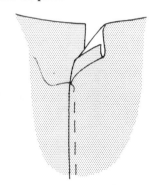

Figure 99

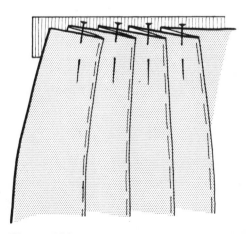

Figure 100

AFTER FITTING

Remove the temporary waistband, making sure that any alterations along the waistline are retained.

Darts

Stitch the darts, from wide end to point. Cut down the centre fold and press apart the two sides to reduce bulk.

All-round pleats

Top-stitch the pleats from the waistline to the hip.

Bound pockets

It is easier to handle a single skirt panel than the whole skirt, so unpick the tacked side seams before setting a bound pocket. (As they are often set across or below darts, these pockets cannot safely be made before fitting the skirt.)

1 With right sides together, tack the pocket to the skirt section, matching the pocket markings.

2 Stitch above and below the pocket marking and across its ends, as one continuous seam.

Pivot at the corners and overlap the last few stitches over the first (*Figure 101*). The distance of the stitching from the pocket markings, 0·6 – 0·8 cm, will be the finished width of the binding. The stitching at the ends should run exactly across the ends of the pocket marking.

3 Cut through both thicknesses along the pocket marking, and snip into the corners (*Figure 102*).

4 Turn the pocket through to the wrong side. Press the two lips of the pocket to meet at the centre of the slit, and press the turnings at each end outwards from the pocket to form tiny pleats (*Figure 103*).

5 Stab-stitch all round the pocket, on the seamline, to secure the binding above and below the opening (*Figure 104*).

6 Press the back of the pocket down to match its edges to the pocket front. Fold the skirt out of the way and stitch round the pocket bag as shown in *Figure 105*, beginning and ending at the ends of the pocket mouth.

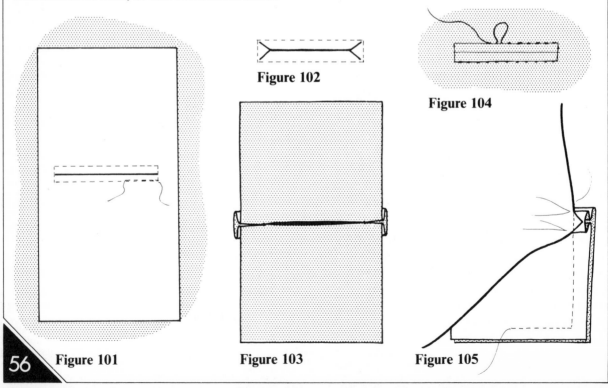

Figure 102

Figure 104

Figure 101

Figure 103

Figure 105

Patch pockets

1 Press 3 cm along the pocket top to the right side. Press the 1·5 cm seam allowance at the top of the pocket lining to the wrong side (*Figure 106*).

2 Place pocket and lining right sides together as shown in *Figure 107*. Stitch the seam round the pocket. Trim the corners.

3 Turn the pocket right-side-out through the opening at the top of the lining. Slip-hem the top fold of the lining to the pocket.

Patch pockets with flaps

Press half the width of the flap, above the shaping, to the right side (*Figure 108*); then continue as above.

Patch pockets with shaped openings

Match pocket and lining with right sides together and stitch all round, leaving a small opening at the side. Trim corners, clip curves, turn right-side-out and press (*Figure 109*).

Attaching patch pockets

Tack the pocket in place and top-stitch close to its side and lower edges, beginning and ending with a small square or triangle of stitching (*Figure 110*); or attach invisibly by back-stitching through the skirt from the wrong side.

Side seams

Stitch and press open the side seams, leaving the opening for the zip. If the seams include panel pockets, or have patch pockets taken into them as in *Figure 68(c)* and (*e*), stitch straight along the seamline through all thicknesses.

If there is a plain seamline pocket as in *Figure 68(a)*, stitch the seam round the pocket bag without a break, pivoting at the top and bottom of the pocket opening. Clip the turnings so that the seam can be pressed open and the pocket pressed towards the front.

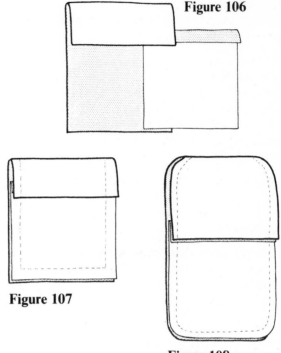

Figure 106

Figure 107

Figure 108

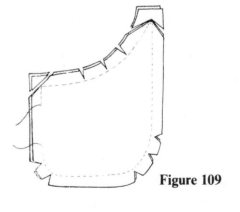

Figure 109

Figure 110

The zip: plain setting

1 Tack together the sides of the opening along the seamline. Press the turnings open.

2 Pin the zip under the tacked seamline. If you pin from the right side, you can feel the position of the zipper chain through the fabric; pin it either centrally or slightly towards the left of the seam. Tack where you have pinned (*Figure 111*).

3 Working from the wrong side, with a zipper foot on the machine, stitch down the centre of one tape, across the bottom below the teeth, and up the other side (*Figure 112*). Remove the tackings.

The zip: concealed setting in side seam
See the right and wrong side photographs on page 48.

1 Finish the edges of the opening extensions with zigzag stitching.

2 Mark with chalk the seamline on the back section of the skirt, A–B in *Figure 113*.

3 Press back the extension 1 cm beyond the chalked line.

4 Pin the zip behind the fold, with the top of the chain a good 1·5 cm below the top edge of the fabric.

5 Cut a zip-guard the length of the extension and 6 cm wide. Finish its sides and lower end with zigzag stitching. Centre it behind the zip, and tack.

6 With a zipper foot on the machine, stitch close to the fold (*Figure 114*).

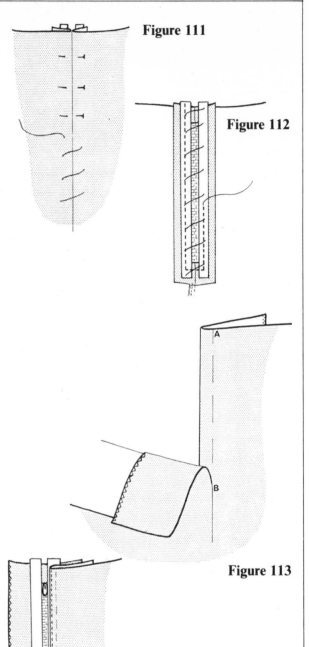

Figure 111

Figure 112

Figure 113

Figure 114

7 Turn to the wrong side and stitch together the turnings of skirt and guard, through the enclosed edge of the zipper tape.

8 Pin the skirt front over the zip, matching the seam lines. Tack the folded edges together (*Figure 115*).

9 Fold the zip-guard out of the way. Tack and top-stitch down the front of the opening, through the two thicknesses of fabric and the zipper tape. Curve the stitching across below the end-stop of the zip.

10 Now, with the zip-guard folded back again to its proper place, stitch through all thicknesses to the seamline.

11 Through the front extension only, run a second row of machining down the front zipper tape for extra strength.

Snap-fasteners
In an all-round pleated skirt, dispense with a zip; the opening will be at the back of a pleat where it is awkward to set a zip smoothly. Use snap-fasteners instead – they will give a clean line and save you trouble. Close the waistband with a hook and bar as usual.

Front facings for wrapover skirts
Interface the facing. Seam the facing to the front edge of the skirt, notch the seam turnings so that they will lie flat, turn the facing to the inside and press. Top-stitching, as in the photograph on page 39, makes a good finish, but should be worked all round after the hem is turned up.

A facing cut in one with the skirt should be interfaced as far as the fold, then simply be turned in and pressed.

FINISHING THE SKIRT
The lining
Stitch the seams and darts of the lining. If the skirt fabric is likely to 'seat', the lining can be made fractionally tighter than the skirt itself by stitching 2 cm (instead of 1·5 cm) from the edges of the side seams only. This will tighten the lining by a total of 2 cm. Turn up and machine the hem.

With *wrong* sides together, match the lining to the skirt and tack them together round the waist. Fold in the lining seam allowances down the sides of the opening and fell them to the zipper tapes (*Figure 116*).

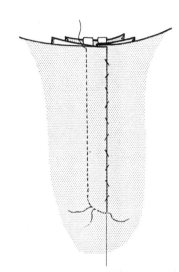

Figure 115

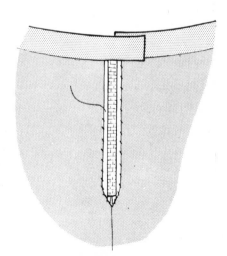

Figure 116

The waistband

A straight waistband should be stiffened with iron-on interfacing across half its width (not across its facing).

1 Trim off a scant 1 cm along the facing edge, and finish it with zigzag stitching.

2 Stitch the short seams at each end of the waistband, stopping short of the seam allowance. Trim and turn the band right-side-out.

3 With right sides together, match the waistband notches to the skirt seams, letting the extension come at the back of the opening to correspond with the zip-guard, if any (*Figure 117*).

4 Stitch the waist seam.

5 Press the turnings and the ends of the zipper tapes up inside the waistband. Tack the waistband facing in place so that its zigzagged edge comes just below the seamline. From the right side, top-stitch exactly along the seamline to catch in the edge of the waistband facing. This stitching will sink invisibly into the seamline. *Figure 118* shows the right and wrong sides.

Shaped waistbands have a seam along their top edge. Interface the waistband; then with right sides together stitch it to its facing along the upper edge and ends. Turn right-side-out and press. Continue as for straight waistbands.

Petersham finish

Cut the petersham to the length of the waistline, plus a turning of 1 cm at each end.

With the petersham on the wrong side of the skirt, match its edge to the waist seamline. From the wrong side, stitch close to this edge. *Figure 119* shows the right side.

Trim and cover the raw edges with seam binding.

Fold the petersham to the inside of the skirt; attached in this way, no white edge of petersham can show along the top of the skirt.

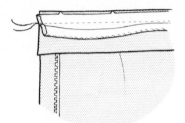

Figure 117

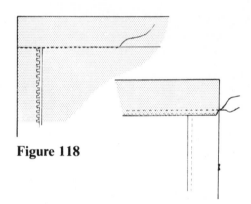

Figure 118

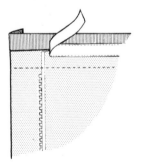

Figure 119

MAKING UP THE SKIRT

Waistline hook and bar

With either waist finish, take the strain off the zip and make a firm waistline by using a heavy hook and bar (*Figure 120*). Wrapover skirts also need an inside hook to hold up the underwrap.

Waistline facings

Interface and seam together the facing pieces. Finish the lower edge with zigzag stitching.

With right sides together, tack the facing to the skirt waistline matching the seams and the opening. Include a length of narrow tape in this seam, to prevent any stretching (*Figure 121*). Stitch the seam.

Turn the facing to the inside, turn in the ends and fell them to the zipper tapes. Finish with a hook and bar.

The hem finish

All hems should be lightly pressed at the fold. Do not press over the stitched edge of the hem, as you may leave a ridge mark on the right side.

With binding

Use seam binding on straight skirts. Machine one edge of the binding to the hem turning. Hem the other edge to the skirt (*Figure 122*).

On a flared skirt use bias binding which will stretch round the curve of the hem. Open out one crease of the binding. Machine it along the crease to the hem turning. Fold upwards and slip-hem the other fold to the skirt (*Figure 123*).

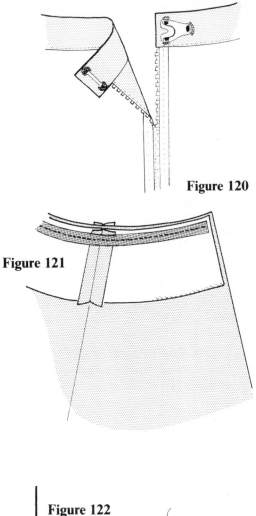

Figure 120

Figure 121

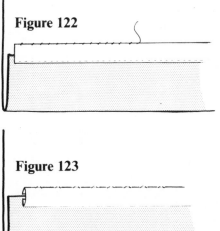

Figure 122

Figure 123

MAKING UP THE SKIRT

With the blind-hemming stitch
This stitch is built into automatic and
semi-automatic sewing machines (*Figure 124*).

1 Finish the edge of the hem turning with
zigzag stitching.

2 Tack the hem turning in place (*Figure 125*).

3 Fold back the hem along the line of tacking
(*Figure 126*).

4 Work the blind-hemming stitch on the edge
of the turning. Let the straight stitches fall on
the single thickness of fabric, and the
swing-stitch just bite into the fold. If you work
too far from the fold, the swing-stitch will
miss it altogether; if you are too close to it,
long vertical stitches like exclamation marks
will appear on the right side. It is worth trying
this stitch on a scrap of fabric until you can
judge the exact distance that will produce
tiny, inconspicuous stitches on the right side
(*Figure 127*).

Pleated hemlines
Turn up the hem all round, tack and finish
with binding or blind-stitching. Press in the
lower ends of the pleats *after* you have
worked the hem.

If a skirt seam falls at the back of a pleat,
avoid bulk in the hem as follows.

Figure 124

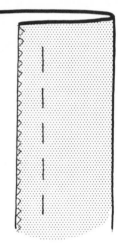

Figure 125

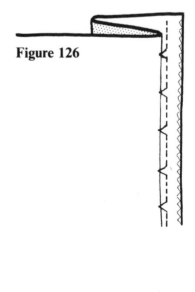

Figure 126

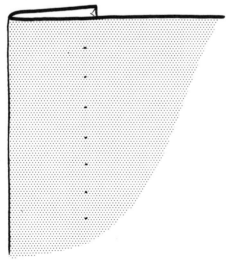

Figure 127

MAKING UP THE SKIRT

1 Unpick the seam for the depth of the hem turning (*Figure 128*).

2 Turn up and work separately the section of hem between each seam (*Figure 129*).

3 Stitch the skirt seam from above the hem (overlapping a few stitches) down to the folded edges. Back-stitch for strength (*Figure 130*).

4 Clip the seam turnings above the hem, and trim them narrowly down the hem itself (*Figure 131*).

5 Oversew these narrow edges closely and firmly together. They will be invisible inside the skirt, and the pleat will lie quite flat at the hem (*Figure 132*).

Fully flared hemlines
The wider the flare, the narrower the hem should be. Finish with bias binding.

Loosely-woven fabrics, and some jerseys, will tend to drop unevenly if the skirt is circular or very fully flared. So hang it from its waistline for a week; the parts where the hemline is on the bias of the weave may drop considerably. Re-mark a level hemline, trim and finish with bias binding.

Frilled or flounced hemlines
First, join the sections and work the hem of the flounce or frill. (A frill can be doubled in half to give a painless, ready-finished edge.)

Gather the raw edges if necessary. With right sides together, stitch the flounce or frill to the skirt. Trim the seam turnings and machine them together with zigzag stitching. Fold the frill downwards (*Figure 133*).

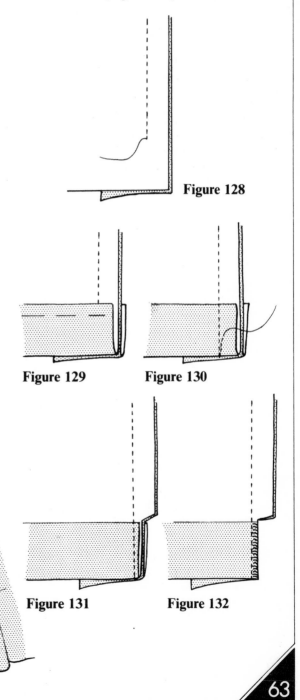

Figure 128

Figure 129   Figure 130

Figure 131   Figure 132

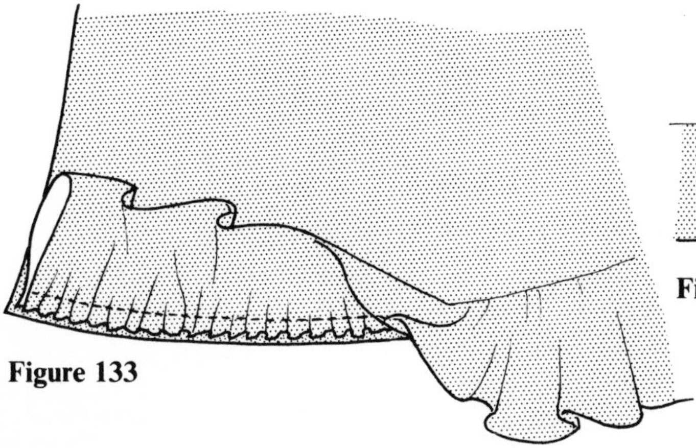

Figure 133

MAKING UP THE SKIRT

Hem for wrapover skirts
Turn up and work the hem. Turn in the facing over the hem. Herringbone the edge of the facing to the hem (*Figure 134*).

Arrowheads
These can be worked as a decorative strengthening at the tops of pleats. Mark the triangular outline with chalk. Work the arrowhead with buttonhole twist, keeping the stitches closely together.

Bring the needle up at the bottom left-hand corner, and take a tiny stitch across the top. Take the next stitch across the base and continue with longer stitches across the top and shorter ones across the base until the triangle is filled (*Figure 135*).

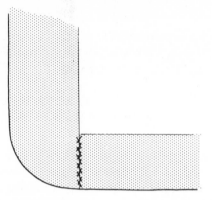

Figure 134

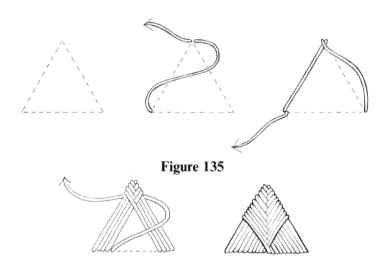

Figure 135